MW01100388

WordPerfect® for Windows™

Wiley Command Reference

Wiley Command References are designed for intermediate to advanced users of computer applications. These fast and easy-to-use sourcebooks give you the essential information you need to carry out commands quickly and concisely. Other Wiley Command References include:

Lotus 1-2-3 for Windows Command Reference, E. Michael Lunsford

DOS 5 Command Reference, Ken W. Christopher, Jr., Barry A. Feigenbaum, and Shon O. Saliga

Paradox for Windows Command Reference, Jonathan Kamin

Paradox 3.5 Command Reference, Jonathan Kamin

Quattro Pro for Windows Command Reference, Jennifer Meyer

Quattro Pro 3 Command Reference, Jennifer Meyer

NetWare Command Reference, Marci Andrews and Elizabeth L. Wilcox

Signature Command Reference, Christine Rivera

Q&A 4 Command Reference, Karim Meghji and Dave Reid

Microsoft Word 5.5 Command Reference, Pam Beason

DOS 4 Command Reference, Ken W. Christopher, Jr., Barry A. Feigenbaum, and Shon O. Saliga

To order your Command References, you can call Wiley directly at (212) 469-4400 or check your local bookstores.

WordPerfect® for Windows™

Wiley Command Reference

Jennifer Foster

John Wiley & Sons, Inc.

New York • Chichester • Brisbane • Toronto • Singapore

In recognition of the importance of preserving what has been written, it is a policy of John Wiley & Sons, Inc. to have books of enduring value published in the United States printed on acid-free paper, and we exert our best efforts to that end.

Library of Congress Cataloging-in-Publication Data

Foster, Jennifer (Jennifer J.)
    WordPerfect for Windows command reference / Jennifer Foster.
        p.   cm.
    Includes index.
    ISBN 0-471-54902-9 (paper)
    1. Word processing—Computer programs.   2. WordPerfect (Computer program)   3. Windows (Computer programs)   I. Title.
    Z52.5.W65F67   1992
    652.5'536—dc20   91-43508
                                                                            CIP

Printed and bound by Courier Companies, Inc.
10 9 8 7 6 5 4 3 2 1

Contents

Introduction   1

Audience   1
How to Use this Book   2
Organization   2

Conventions Used in this
   Book   3

Chapter 1   WordPerfect for Windows Concepts   5

WordPerfect Concepts   6
Button Bar   6
Draft Mode   7
File Manager   7
Keyboard   8
Reveal Codes   9
Ruler Bar   10
Error Messages   10
Getting Started   11
Open a File   11
Save   12

Close a File   13
Exit WordPerfect   14
Maneuvering in
   WordPerfect   14
Goto   14
Search   15
Select (Block)   16
Undelete   17
Undo   17
Window   18
Shortcuts   19

Chapter 2   Setting System Defaults   21

Backup Options   21
Date, Format   23
Directory, Changing   24
Directory, Default   25
Display Preferences   26
Document Defaults   27
Document Summary,
   Default   28
Draft Mode Colors   29
Environment   30

Equations   31
Initial Codes   33
Keyboard   34
Keyboard Creating   35
Language   36
Location of Files   37
Merge   38
Printer, Initial Settings   39
Reveal Codes Colors   41
Table of Authorities   42

Chapter 3   Manipulating Files   45

Button Bar   45
Clear Screen   46
Close a File   47
Codes, Initial   47
Convert from Other
    Format   48
Copy File   50
Delete Files   51
Document Comments   52
Document Compare   52
Document Summary   53
Draft Mode   54
Exit WordPerfect   55
File Manager Assign
    Applications to Menu   56
File Manager Associate   56
File Manager Attributes   57
File Manager Copy File   58
File Manager Create
    Directory   59
File Manager Delete Files   60

File Manager Information   61
File Manager List Files   62
File Manager Move/
    Rename   63
File Manager Navigator   64
File Manager Print   65
File Manager Print
    Window   66
File Manager Search   67
File Manager View Layout   68
File Manager Viewer   69
Find a File   70
Move/Rename File   71
Open a File   73
Password   73
Quick List   75
Retrieve File   75
Save   76
Save As   77
View   78

Chapter 4   Manipulating the Page   81

Append   81
Block Protect   81
Cancel   82
Conditional End of Page   83
Cut   83
Date, Automatically
    Inserting   84
Deleting Codes   85
Document Summary   86
Enter   87
Envelopes   87
Footnotes/Endnotes   88
Forms   91
Headers/Footers   92

Outline   94
Paragraph Numbering   96
Paper Size   97
Paste   99
Portrait/Landscape   99
Reveal Codes, Using   100
Reveal Codes Window,
    Changing Size   101
Save Block   101
Typeover   102
Undelete   103
Undo   103
Widow/Orphan   104

Chapter 5 Layout 105

Bold *105*
Capitalization of New Text *106*
Center Line *106*
Columns, Newspaper or Parallel *107*
Convert Case *109*
Display Pitch *110*
Flush Right *110*
Font Attributes *111*
Font, Initial *113*
Hanging Paragraph *114*
Hyphenation *115*
Indent *116*
Indent Left and Right *117*
Italics *118*
Justification *118*
Kerning *119*
Line Height *120*
Line Numbering *121*
Line Spacing *122*
Margin Release *123*
Margins *123*

Overstrike *125*
Page Break *126*
Page Numbering *127*
Redline Method *128*
Redline/Strikeout *129*
Ruler Bar *130*
Ruler Bar Columns *131*
Ruler Bar Font and Size *132*
Ruler Bar Justification *133*
Ruler Bar Spacing *134*
Ruler Bar Styles *134*
Ruler Bar Tab *135*
Ruler Bar Tables *136*
Special Codes *136*
Styles *138*
Superscript, Subscript *140*
Suppress Page Format *141*
Tabs, Set *142*
Type Size, Changing *143*
Underline *145*
Underline Spaces or Tabs *145*
WordPerfect Characters *146*

Chapter 6 Search, Replace, Speller, Thesaurus, and Word Count 149

Replace *149*
Search *151*
Search Next *152*
Search Previous *153*

Speller *153*
Thesaurus *155*
Word Count *156*

Chapter 7 Lists and Macros 159

Concordance *159*
Cross-Reference *160*
Index *161*
Lists *163*
Macros, Assigning to Button Bar *165*
Macros, Assigning to Macro Menu *166*
Macros, Converting *167*

Macros, Playing *169*
Macros, Recording *169*
Mark Text *171*
Marked Text, Define *172*
Marked Text, Generate *173*
Master Document *174*
Table of Authorities *176*
Table of Contents *178*

Chapter 8   Merge, Sort, and Labels   181

Labels   *181*   Sort   *186*
Merge   *184*

Chapter 9   Graphics, Equations, Boxes, and Tables   189

Boxes (Table, Text, User)   *190*   Line, Graphic   *199*
Equations   *192*   Tables   *200*
Figure   *195*   Tables, Math   *202*
Line Draw   *197*

Chapter 10   Spreadsheets   203

DDE Link   *203*   Spreadsheet, Link
Spreadsheet, Import   *205*   Options   *207*
Spreadsheet, Link   *206*

Chapter 11   Printing   209

Advance   *210*   Print Manager   *226*
Cancel Print Job   *211*   Print Preview   *227*
Cartridges and Soft Fonts   *212*   Print to Disk   *229*
Center Page   *214*   Printer Commands   *230*
Color Printing   *214*   Printer, Deleting   *231*
Document on Disk, Printing   Printer, Installing   *232*
  from   *215*   Printer, Selecting   *233*
Font, Choosing   *216*   Printer Setup   *234*
Forms, Printing   *218*   Printer Setup (File
Initialize Printer   *219*   Manager)   *235*
Landscape Printing   *219*   Sheet Feeder   *237*
Multiple Files, Printing   *220*   WordPerfect Printer
Multiple Pages, Printing   *221*   Drivers   *239*
Print   *222*   WordPerfect Printer Drivers,
Print Block   *224*   Modifying   *240*
Print, Double Sided   *225*

Appendix A   WordPerfect and Windows   243

Windows Concepts   *244*   Adding WordPerfect to a
System Requirements   *244*   Group in the Program
Basic Maneuvering in   Manager   *246*
  Windows   *245*   Going to DOS   *246*

Opening WordPerfect *247*
Maximizing Memory in
    Windows *247*
CONFIG.SYS File,
    Modifying *249*
Windows Commands in
    WordPerfect *249*
Cascade *250*
Clipboard *250*

Control Menu Box *252*
Tile *253*
Printing *253*
File Manager *254*
Print Manager, Enable/
    Disable *254*
Installing Windows Printer
    Drivers *255*
Windows Printer Drivers,
    Installing *255*

Glossary   **259**

Index   **263**

Introduction

Except for the way it looks and feels, WordPerfect for Windows is the same WordPerfect you know and love. However, WordPerfect for Windows looks and feels considerably different than previous WordPerfect versions.

Whether this is good or bad depends on how much you use other Windows applications. If your computer life centers around Windows, you will find that WordPerfect has—finally—joined the Windows revolution. All the features you expect from WordPerfect, plus several enhancements, are at last in a standardized Windows package.

On the other hand, if you are a long-time WordPerfect user and only go to your Windows applications to play solitaire or Reversi, you have a period of adjustment coming. While the WordPerfect features are the same, the way to get to those functions has changed, making it difficult for those of us whose fingers used to be able to manipulate a WordPerfect document without input from the brain.

Audience

This book is intended as a quick reference guide for those familiar with WordPerfect's features or willing to check two or three places to find a feature. If you do not know WordPerfect's terminology, telling you how to use *Sort*, for example, will not help, even with a description of what Sort does. You have to know a feature exists before you start to look for it.

How to Use this Book ⎯⎯⎯⎯⎯⎯⎯

As a quick reference guide this book is designed to help you find and use a feature quickly.

Each feature and command is described by function: for example, the print commands are listed together in one chapter, and commands relating to macros are described in another. Every command and feature is also listed and cross-referenced in the index, giving you several places to check when you are looking for a particular function.

Organization ⎯⎯⎯⎯⎯⎯⎯⎯⎯

This book is organized by WordPerfect's functions, corresponding roughly to the Menu Bar.

- **Chapter 1** tells you how to set up WordPerfect, open, save, and close a document, and exit from the program. This chapter also discusses the new Button Bar, File Manager, and Quick List applications, as well as the CUA/WordPerfect 5.1 keyboard options.

- **Chapter 2** shows you how to set the system defaults to your specifications. (This is not the same thing as installation. System defaults include how often you want the documents backed up and what color you want for Draft Mode.)

- **Chapter 3** helps you manipulate files: save them to different formats, add passwords, compare screen to disk version, and copy, rename, move, and delete the documents that you work with.

- **Chapter 4** helps you manipulate the page: add headers or footers, center the page, add footnotes and endnotes, cut and paste text, automatically insert dates, number paragraphs, and change the paper size.

- **Chapter 5** shows you how to use the formatting and style sheet features: how to set tabs and margins, indent, create columns, work with type, and use the Ruler Bar to greatest advantage.

- **Chapter 6** helps you use some of WordPerfect's tools—the speller, thesaurus, and word count features—and shows you how to use the search and replace functions.

- **Chapter 7** discusses macros and lists, tables of contents and authorities, cross-references, and indexes.

- **Chapter 8** shows you how to use the merge and sort features and how to create labels.

- **Chapter 9** focuses on what WordPerfect refers to as graphics: not only illustrations, but scientific equations, boxes of different types, and tables.

- **Chapter 10** shows you how to use spreadsheets. Although you cannot create them with WordPerfect, you can edit and format them and link their data to a source document, ensuring constantly updated information.

- **Chapter 11** lists the print commands that you can use in WordPerfect: how to print a block of text, print to disk, change printers, and add or delete fonts.

- **Appendix A** gives an overview of how Windows works: specifically, how to maneuver through Windows and Windows applications, and how Windows and WordPerfect work together.

Conventions Used in this Book

The description of each command in this book includes the keystrokes to use (if they exist), as well as the Menu Bar location. Because WordPerfect for Windows can use either its own proprietary keyboard or the Windows-standard keyboard, called the Common User Access (CUA) keyboard, the keystrokes for each keyboard are identified. If you continue using the WordPerfect 5.1 keyboard, keep in mind that the keystrokes required to access a command in WordPerfect for

Windows are not necessarily the ones you used to access the same command in WordPerfect 5.1.

This book uses the following conventions:

- In the shortcut references at the top of each command, the menu name is given first, with the rest of the pathname in parentheses.

- Characters in brackets, such as <F1> or <Enter>, indicate keyboard functions. "Press <Enter>" means press the <Enter> key, not type E-n-t-e-r. The ← key is the backspace key that deletes as it goes; the left-arrow key is spelled out.

- "Select" indicates the specific menu; "choose" refers to the subheads on the menu.

- Cross-references are to the current chapter unless otherwise specified.

- *Filename* or *File*, in italics, indicates that you should enter the name of your own file.

1

WordPerfect for Windows Concepts

WordPerfect for Windows is a Windows program, and it looks and acts like one. This means the program is mouse-based, with feature access through the Menu Bar at the top of the screen. Although WordPerfect says you can navigate through the program without a mouse, you will not be fully productive if you do not use a mouse. (The easiest and most fun method of familiarizing yourself with the mouse is to play one of the games shipped with your Windows package.)

Like other Windows applications, WordPerfect uses icons to open, save, close, and print documents. Some of the keystrokes that could be used as shortcuts in the MS-DOS version of WordPerfect 5.1 no longer work. You need to learn the new keyboard shortcuts for the functions that you use with every document (open, save, and the like) unless you put these functions on your Button Bar; learning the keystroke shortcuts is not as important for those functions that you use only every so often.

WordPerfect has assigned a number of functions to the <Ctrl> key. Some of these functions have been assigned the same keys on both the Common User Access (CUA) and WordPerfect 5.1 keyboards. They are listed in the *Shortcuts* at the end of this chapter.

If you do not understand the way a WordPerfect command functions, review the Help Menu information about that command. By going to the Help Menu (click on Help in the upper right-hand corner, drag to Index, and then use the search icon at the top of the Help box), you can easily locate information about a particular function. Remember that you may need to practice the command a few times before it makes sense to you.

WordPerfect Concepts _____

WordPerfect has several features that are found in few other word processors. These features include:

- Button Bar
- Draft Mode
- File Manager
- Keyboard
- Reveal Codes

These features, as well as a Ruler Bar that offers several formatting shortcuts, are described next.

Button Bar _____

The Button Bar allows you to bypass the menus and put your most commonly used operations on the top, bottom, or side of your screen. Functions such as printing, spelling, creating headers and footers, saving, and exiting a document or WordPerfect can be placed on this bar for instant access. Any feature found on any of the menus can be put on a Button Bar; you can even add macros. You can create as many Button Bars as you need and select the one that is most appropriate.

You can add as many buttons to the Button Bar as you like. If you have more than nine or so, make the buttons "text only" (changed from the View Menu) so that you can see them all without scrolling.

WordPerfect provides several different Button Bars, each with a separate function: that is, one is for tables, one for graphics, and so on. The wp{wp}.wwb Button Bar, the one you see the first time you activate the Button Bar, is a general purpose bar containing buttons to let you open, close, save, print, and search. If it does not meet your needs, you can edit and rename it.

See Also: **Chapter 3,** *Manipulating Files,* for information on creating or changing a Button Bar.

_____ *Draft Mode*

Draft Mode puts the focus on the text that you are working with,
rather than giving you a what-you-see-is-what-you-get repre-
sentation. In contrast, the Default Mode gives you the larger
picture: fonts, page breaks, margins, and white space are all
accurately portrayed. However, Default Mode is smaller than
life-size, making text smaller than 12-point Courier difficult to
see and use.

In Draft Mode, the type is uniform, no matter what fonts you
have chosen, and margins are nonexistent. This allows you to
concentrate on the file itself and ignore the formatting until you
are ready. When you are through working with the text, you
can switch to the Default Mode to see and manipulate the formatting and typographical features in the document.

See Also: **Chapter 3,** *Manipulating Files,* for information on how to toggle between WordPerfect's
default and draft modes.

_____ *File Manager*

The File Manager is a standalone application that is an expanded
interpretation of the List Files feature found in previous
WordPerfect versions. (List Files, as a feature, is no longer available.) You can use WordPerfect's File Manager as long as you
are in Windows, whether or not you are running WordPerfect.
Windows has a File Manager, too. It does much the same thing
as WordPerfect's File Manager, only for the whole system.

File Manager allows you to open, copy, move, or delete files.
Its Navigator feature allows you to see every subdirectory in
any given directory, manipulating all of the files in the directory
path.

From File Manager, you can also obtain and print system information (the amount of memory on your hard disk, your version of MS-DOS, and what kind of printers you have installed and which one is active). You can also print multiple WordPerfect files without opening them by dragging the mouse to highlight as many files as you want to print.

You can access several other programs through File Manager, among them the thesaurus and the speller, making it easy to use these features outside WordPerfect. (The thesaurus and speller can also be selected from inside WordPerfect, through the Tools Menu.)

Menu Bar: File (File Manager)

CUA
Keyboard: Not Available

WordPerfect
5.1 Keyboard: 〈F5〉

Description: Allows you to manipulate multiple Word-
                   Perfect files.

Procedure: 1. Select the File Menu.

                   2. Choose File Manager.

                   3. You are now in a separate program, al-
                      though still within WordPerfect. When you
                      finish your file operations, return to
                      WordPerfect by using the File/Exit Menu.

See Also: **Chapter 3,** *Manipulating Files,* for specific
                   commands in the File Manager.

Keyboard

The keyboard feature, allowing you to switch between a Windows-standard (CUA) keyboard and a WordPerfect MS-DOS 5.1 keyboard, is designed to make both longtime and new WordPerfect users feel comfortable. It is not a very satisfactory solution.

When WordPerfect added new features to WordPerfect for Windows, it added new function keys. However, the new function keys were not necessarily assigned to the new functions. In many cases, the old function keys have been assigned to new features, while new function keys must be used to access old features. That means you are going to have to learn new function keys no matter which keyboard you use. It also means that the old function keys now do things they never did before, so you will have to unlearn some function keys as well. (If you are a longtime WordPerfect user and switch to the CUA keyboard, <F1> is going to drive you crazy. Instead of canceling something, <F1> now puts you into the Help Menu.)

The best solution is to learn the CUA keyboard from the beginning. Once you know the keyboard, you can then use any program that uses the same keyboard, and more of those applications exist every day. An added advantage to learning the CUA keyboard is that keyboard shortcuts (shown on the Menus) are for the CUA keyboard. They may not work if you use the WordPerfect 5.1 keyboard.

WordPerfect for Windows ships with the CUA keyboard active, but during installation it asks which keyboard you want. No matter what your decision, you can switch back and forth between the two at any time.

See Also: **Chapter 2,** *Setting System Defaults,* for information on how to change the keyboard setting.

_____*Reveal Codes*

WordPerfect, unlike most other word processors, allows you to see on a separate screen the codes that it is putting in your document. This feature is extremely helpful when you are trying to figure out why a line or page does not behave properly: for example, it shows exactly where you inserted a font, thus explaining why two words are in different typefaces. You can manipulate the codes (move, copy, or delete them) through the keyboard. In previous versions of WordPerfect, the Reveal Codes feature was very frustrating for beginning users, who would often find themselves trapped in the Reveal Codes screen without understanding how they got there or how they could get out. Reveal Codes can be accessed through the Menu Bar now, although <Alt><F3> still works for both keyboards.

See Also: **Chapter 4,** *Manipulating the Page,* for information on how to use Reveal Codes.

Ruler Bar _____

The ruler, new with this version of WordPerfect, has some extremely convenient features. You can create new tab settings by dragging the tab mark below the ruler to the spot on the ruler where you want a tab, and you can assign fonts (through the Font Menu) to the ruler for faster access. Other shortcut buttons are for styles, tables, columns, justification, and line spacing. If you can accept the Ruler Bar default (columns, for example, are newspaper-style only), you can save a lot of time.

See Also: *Environment* (Chapter 2) to change the ruler default settings.

In Chapter 5, see *Ruler Bar* to toggle the Ruler on and off and *Ruler Bar Columns, Ruler Bar Fonts, Ruler Bar Spacing, Ruler Bar Justification, Ruler Bar Tables,* and *Ruler Bar Styles* to use the shortcuts offered by this feature.

Error Messages _____

Error messages pop up in the middle of your screen. Most of them are informational, requiring no more action on your part than clicking on OK.

Other messages are more serious, and it may require some effort on your part to prevent them from happening again. "Terminating Application," for example, means that you are leaving WordPerfect immediately, with none of your open files saved. (This is the best reason for setting your timed, automatic backup to a frequent interval.) These kinds of messages generally indicate memory problems or, possibly, less than optimal setup of Windows. Write down the circumstances when these messages occur and have your computer person check your setup. If the problem persists, call WordPerfect.

Getting Started

This section describes the commands that you need to manipulate a WordPerfect file—how to open, save, and close it—as well as how to exit from WordPerfect. Also in this section are the ways to maneuver in a WordPerfect document: getting to the beginning or end of the page or file and blocking ("Selecting") a word, paragraph, or page to cut and paste, move, or copy.

WordPerfect for Windows is accessed the same way that other Windows applications are accessed, by calling up Windows, then double-clicking on the WordPerfect icon. This takes you to a screen titled "Document1—Unmodified." If you are creating a new document, you can begin. If you want to work on a preexisting file, you must first open it.

Remember as you work in WordPerfect that all commands work forward unless specifically stated otherwise: that is, if you change margins at the top of page two, the margins are not changed for page one.

Open a File

Menu Bar: File (Open)

**CUA
Keyboard:**   <F4>

WordPerfect
5.1 Keyboard: <Shift><F10>

Description: Allows you to open already-created files.

Procedure: 1. Select the File Menu.

2. Choose Open.

3. You are in the wpwin directory. To change directories, double-click on the [..] icon in the right-hand box, which will take you to the parent directory and show you all the subdirectories in that root directory. (If the box does not contain the [..] icon, click on the Quick List box at the bottom of the screen.)

4. Double-click on the desired subdirectory. The files in that directory will appear in the left-hand box.

5. Double-click on the desired file.

Shortcut: At the bottom of the File Menu are the last four files you saved. Click on any of them instead of retrieving the file from the directory.

See Also: *Draft Mode* (Chapter 3), *Quick List* (Chapter 3).

Save _____

Menu Bar: File (Save)

CUA
Keyboard: <Shift><F3>

MS-DOS
Keyboard: <F10>

Description: Allows you to save a file.

Procedure: 1. Select the File Menu.

2. Choose Save. If the file has never been saved, a menu box will prompt you to give the file an 11-character name, including the extension. If the file already has a name, it will be automatically saved.

Notes: 1. To save a file to another directory, with another name, or in a different format, use the Save As command.

2. Do not used the Timed Backup feature in place of a formal Save. Timed Backup files are deleted when you exit properly from WordPerfect. In addition, the Timed Backup feature does not distinguish between the file you are working on now and the file you worked on 15 minutes ago in the same window; the latest Timed Backup overwrites all previous Timed Backup files for that window.

See Also: *Save As* (Chapter 3).

_____ *Close a File*

Menu Bar: File (Close)

CUA Keyboard: \<Ctrl\>\<F4\>

WordPerfect 5.1 Keyboard: \<F7\>

Description: Allows you to close a file and clear the screen.

Procedure: 1. Select the File Menu.

2. Choose Close. If no changes have been made to the file since it was last saved, the screen will clear. If changes have been

made, a box prompts you to save the changes.

Exit WordPerfect _____

Menu Bar:	File (Exit)
CUA Keyboard:	<Alt><F4>
WordPerfect 5.1 Keyboard:	<F7>
Description:	Allows you to exit from WordPerfect.
Procedure:	1. Select the File Menu.
	2. Choose Exit. If no changes have been made to the open file since it was last saved, you will be returned to the Windows Program Manager or Desktop. If changes have been made, a box prompts you to save the changes before leaving the program.
Shortcut:	Double-click on the Control Menu box (upper left-hand corner of the WordPerfect screen.)
See Also:	*Control Menu Box* (Appendix A).

Maneuvering in WordPerfect _____

Goto _____

Menu Bar:	Edit (Goto)
Function Keys:	<Ctrl><G>

Description: Allows you to go to any specified page in the document that is currently open on the screen.

WordPerfect
Default: Current page

Procedure: 1. Select Goto from anywhere in your document.

   2. A box appears prompting you for the page number you want. Enter the number.

   3. Click on OK.

   4. To return to the original page, select Goto again and click on Last Position.

Note: If you want to go to the top or bottom of the *current* page, use the scroll bar on the Position box to select that option.

See Also: *Search*

_____ *Search*

Menu Bar: Edit (Search)

Function
Keys: <F2>

Description: Allows you to search forward or backward for a specified text string.

Procedure: 1. Select Edit from anywhere in your document.

   2. Click on Search.

   3. In the box, enter the text string you are searching for.

   4. If you are searching for WordPerfect codes:

      a. Click on the Codes box.

        b. Scroll through the list of codes, high-
           lighting the one or ones you need.

        c. Click on Insert to make the code part of
           the text string.

5. If you want to limit the search to the document body (and not include headers,
   footers, or indexing, for example), click on
   Search on Document Body Only.

6. If you want to search backwards from the
   current cursor location, click and drag on
   the direction box until Backward appears.

7. When all options have been resolved satisfactorily, click on OK to begin the search.
   WordPerfect will find the next instance of
   the text string.

See Also: *Replace* (Chapter 6).

Select (Block) _____

Menu Bar:	Edit (Select, Sentence or Paragraph)
Mouse:	Click and Drag
CUA Keyboard:	⟨F8⟩
WordPerfect 5.1 Keyboard:	⟨Alt⟩⟨F4⟩
Description:	Allows you to select text to move, copy, and/ or delete.
Procedure:	1. Select the Edit Menu.
	2. Choose Select.
	3. Choose Sentence or Paragraph. The sentence or paragraph will be highlighted, allowing you to manipulate it with other Edit Menu commands.

Note: Use the mouse to highlight short amounts of
              text (a line or so); use the keyboard com-
              mands in conjunction with Page Up and Page
              Down to highlight long amounts of text (a
              page or to the end of the document).

_____ *Undelete*

Menu Bar: Edit (Undelete)

**CUA
Keyboard:**   \<Alt\>\<Shift\>←

**WordPerfect
5.1 Keyboard:** \<F3\>

Description: Allows you to retrieve up to your last three
              deletions.

Procedure: 1. Select the Edit Menu.
              2. Choose Undelete. Your most recently de-
                 leted text will appear highlighted on the
                 screen. A box will prompt you to restore
                 this deletion or see the previous deletion.
              3. Press Restore to retrieve the deletion you
                 want.

See Also: *Undo*

_____ *Undo*

Menu Bar: Edit, Undo

**CUA
Keyboard:**   \<Alt\>← or \<Ctrl\>\<Z\>

**WordPerfect
5.1 Keyboard:** \<Ctrl\>\<Z\>

Description: Allows you to reinstate your last change.

Procedure: 1. Select the Edit Menu.

                 2. Choose Undo. Your very last action (typed words, a deletion) will be reversed. For example, if you deleted a word, that word will appear; if you typed a word, it will disappear.

See Also: *Undelete*.

Window

Menu Bar: Window

**CUA
Keyboard:**   <Ctrl><F6> (Next Document)
<Ctrl><Shift><F6> (Previous Document)

**WordPerfect
5.1 Keyboard:**   <Alt><Shift><F6> (Next Window)

Description: Allows you to switch among multiple (up to 12) WordPerfect documents.

Procedure: 1. Select Window. Open files are listed at the bottom of the menu. The one with a check next to it is the currently active window.

                 2. Double-click on any document at the bottom of the window to switch to that document.

                 3. To switch back to your original document, repeat steps 1 and 2.

Note: You can use the Cascade and Tile commands to arrange the active documents so that you can see them all simultaneously.

_____ *Shortcuts*

The following key assignments allow you to move quickly
through WordPerfect documents.

Function	CUA/WP5.1 Keyboard
Cancel	⟨Esc⟩
Undo	⟨Ctrl⟩Z
Cut	⟨Ctrl⟩X
Copy	⟨Ctrl⟩C
Paste	⟨Ctrl⟩V
Bold	⟨Ctrl⟩B
Italics	⟨Ctrl⟩I
Underline	⟨Ctrl⟩U
Normal	⟨Ctrl⟩N
Delete to End of Line	⟨Ctrl⟩⟨Delete⟩
Hard (Forced) Page Break	⟨Ctrl⟩⟨Enter⟩
WordPerfect Character Sets	⟨Ctrl⟩W
Print Document	⟨Ctrl⟩P
Column Left/Right	⟨Alt⟩Left/Right Arrow
Page Up	⟨Page Up⟩
Page Down	⟨Page Down⟩

	CUA Keyboard	WP 5.1 Keyboard
Top of Document	⟨Ctrl⟩⟨Home⟩	⟨Home⟩, ⟨Home⟩↑
Bottom of Document	⟨Ctrl⟩⟨End⟩	⟨Home⟩, ⟨Home⟩↓

2

Setting System Defaults

This chapter deals with customizing WordPerfect to your needs, such as where you want WordPerfect to store files or how often you want to back up your open files. Default settings are listed for each command.

Each of these functions take effect as soon as you enable them, and they remain enabled until you specifically disable them.

Auto Redisplay

See *Display Preferences.*

Backup Files

See *Location of Files.*

Backup Options

Menu Bar:	File (Preferences, Backup)
CUA Keyboard:	\<Ctrl\>\<Shift\>\<F1\>
WordPerfect 5.1 Keyboard:	Not Available
Description:	Allows your open files to be automatically saved at preselected intervals to the directory of your choosing. Each open window has a separate backup file.

WordPerfect

Default: Back up every 20 minutes to the directory that contains your WordPerfect application files.

Procedure: 1. Select the File Menu from anywhere in WordPerfect.

2. Choose Preferences.

3. Choose Backup.

4. Use the scroll bar to choose a new time. You can also enter the time you want between backups. The new setting will remain in effect until you change it. If you do not want timed backup, click on the Timed Backup box to remove the X.

5. Choose Original Document Backup if you want the original document saved with a different extension every time you replace it (either through saving the file or exiting the program). The new setting will remain in effect until you change it.

6. Click OK to save all the changes and exit.

Notes: 1. This timed backup is deleted when you exit WordPerfect properly, so it is not a substitute for saving your files. Timed Backup is designed to protect you in the event of a power outage.

2. Original Document Backup is designed for those with large disks or good housekeeping habits, since you are in essence saving each file twice.

3. To change the location of the backup files, see *Location of Files.*

See Also: *Document Compare* (Chapter 3).

Beep Options

See *Environment*.

Button Bars File Location

See *Location of Files*.

Code Deletion, Confirm On

See *Environment*.

Columns, Display Side by Side

See *Display Preferences*.

Date, Format

Menu Bar:	File (Preferences, Date Format)
CUA Keyboard:	<Ctrl><Shift><F1>
WordPerfect 5.1 Keyboard:	Not Available
Description:	Allows you to change the format of the date that can be automatically inserted into your document.
WordPerfect Default:	Month, Day, Year.
Procedure:	1. Select File from anywhere in WordPerfect.
	2. Choose Preferences.
	3. Choose Date Format.

4. Click on Predefined Dates to select one of the standard date formats, or click on Date Codes or Time Codes to create your own format.

5. Click on OK to save the changes. The date will now automatically print in the new format you established.

Note: The date will not automatically print unless you insert a date code into your document.

See Also: *Date, Automatically Inserting* (Chapter 4).

Dialog Boxes, Display Sculptured _____

See *Display Preferences.*

Directory, Changing _____

Menu Bar: File (Open)

CUA Keyboard: <F4>

WP 5.1 Keyboard: <Shift><F10>

Description: Allows you to designate a new default directory.

Procedure:
1. Select File from a blank screen.
2. Click on Change Default Directory. This will confirm to WordPerfect that the new directory is to be the default.
3. Double-click on [..] to go to the parent directory.

4. Use the mouse to scroll through the subdirectories until you find the one you want. Double-click on the desired directory.

5. Double-click on the desired file.

Notes:

1. If you use the directory frequently, you can add it to the Quick List for faster access.

2. Changing the default directory does not change the location of the auxiliary files. The location of these files must be changed specifically.

See Also: *Directory, Default; Location of Files; Quick List* (Chapter 3).

Directory, Default

Menu Bar: File (Open)

CUA Keyboard: <F4>

WP 5.1 Keyboard: <Shift><F10>

Description: The default directory, identified at the beginning of each WordPerfect session, is where all WordPerfect application files are stored. All files in WordPerfect are automatically saved to the default directory unless a complete pathname precedes the name of the file being saved.

Note: The default is easily changed for each session, although it reverts back to the original default whenever you exit WordPerfect. However, changing the default directory does not change the location of the auxiliary files, which are located in the default directory unless specifically changed.

See Also: *Location of Files; Directory, Changing.*

Display Preferences _____

Menu Bar:	File (Preferences, Display)
CUA Keyboard:	<Ctrl><Shift><F1>
WordPerfect 5.1 Keyboard:	Not Available
Description:	Allows you to view and change any of the default settings from anywhere in Word-Perfect.

Table 2.1.   Default Display Settings

Display Setting	Default
Text in Windows System Colors	On
Auto Redisplay in Draft Mode	On
Display Merge Codes	On
Display Hard Return Character as	None
Display Horizontal Scroll Bar	Off
Status Bar Display	Inches
Graphics in Black and White	Off
Display Columns Side by Side	On
Sculptured Dialog Boxes	Off
Display Vertical Scroll Bar	On
Display and Entry of Numbers	Inches

Procedure: 1. Select File.

2. Choose Preferences.

3. Choose Display.

4. Click on the option you wish to modify, adding or deleting the X in the appropriate boxes to change the toggle. The new set-

ting will remain in effect until you change it.

5. Click on OK to save the changes and exit.

Notes: 1. You can change all of the options at once.

2. Sculptured Dialog Boxes are not available if you have an EGA or monochrome monitor.

Document Defaults

Menu Bar: Layout (Document)

**CUA
Keyboard:**   <Ctrl><Shift><F9>

**WordPerfect
5.1 Keyboard:**   <Shift><F8>

Description: Allows you to modify the file attributes (font, initial codes, redline method) for each document.

Table 2.2.   Document Defaults

New Document Attributes	New Document Defaults
Summary	None
Initial Fonts	12-point Courier
Initial Codes	None*
Redline Method	Printer Dependent
Display Pitch	Automatic

*The system default for initial codes is Justification Left, but this does not show up in the document default.

Procedure: 1. Select Layout on a blank screen.

2. Choose Document.

3. Click on the option you want to change.

4. Make whatever changes you think necessary. Click on OK to save to changes and
return to the document.

Note: Settings made from the Layout Menu must be
made for each document. Settings are overridden by any attributes that have already been
assigned to the document.

See Also: *Document Summary, Default; Initial Codes.*

Document Files Location _____

See *Location of Files.*

Document Summary, Default _____

Menu Bar: File (Preferences, Document Summary)

**CUA
Keyboard:** <Ctrl><Shift><F1>

**WordPerfect
5.1 Keyboard:** Not Available

Description: Allows WordPerfect to automatically prompt
you to create a summary of your file when
you save or exit the document.

**WordPerfect
Default:** Off

Procedure:
1. Select the File Menu from anywhere in
WordPerfect.

2. Choose Document Summary.

3. Click on Create Summary in the Save/Exit
box to change the default.

4. Enter a text string for WordPerfect to
search and include in its summary. RE: is

the default. (WordPerfect searches for RE: and copies up to 160 characters, or to the hard return following RE:, into the summary.)

5. Enter a default description type if you want that information to be included.

6. Click on OK to save the changes and exit from the Document Summary menu.

Note: You can later create document summaries for files that did not originally have them.

See Also: *Document Summary* (Chapter 3).

Document Window Settings

See *Display Preferences.*

Draft Mode Colors

Menu Bar: File (Preferences, Display, Draft Mode Colors)

CUA Keyboard: <Ctrl><Shift><F1>

WordPerfect 5.1 Keyboard: Not Available

Description: Allows you to change the Draft Mode type color and background colors (within the limits of your monitor).

Procedure:
1. Select the File Menu from anywhere in WordPerfect.
2. Choose Preferences.
3. Choose Display.
4. Choose Draft Mode Colors.
5. Click on the attribute you want to change (appearance, type sizes, or other.)

6. Click on the foreground and/or background color whose appearance you want to change in the Draft Mode screen. (You can click on Reset to return the screen to its original appearance.)

7. Click on OK to save the changes and exit.

Note: You cannot change the color attributes of the Default Mode screen.

Environment

Menu Bar: File (Preferences, Environment)

**CUA
Keyboard:**   <Ctrl><Shift><F1>

**WordPerfect
5.1 Keyboard:**   Not Available

Description: Allows WordPerfect to change a number of personal preference items.

Table 2.3.   Environment Defaults

Environment Setting	Default
Auto Code Placement	On
Fast Save	On
Format Retrieved Documents for Default Printer	On
Show Ruler Guides	On
Auto Ruler Display	On
Beep on Hyphenation	On
Hyphenation	External
Display Menu Shortcut Keys	On
Confirm on Code Deletion	On
	(continued)

Table 2.3. Environment Defaults *(continued)*

Environment Setting	Default
Allow Undo	On
Tabs Snap to Ruler Guide	On
Ruler Button on Top	Off
Beep on Error	Off
Prompt for Hyphenation	When required
Beep on Search Failure	Off
Display Last Open Filenames	On

Procedure:
1. Select the File Menu from anywhere in WordPerfect.
2. Choose Preferences.
3. Choose Environment.
4. Click on the options you wish to modify, adding or deleting the X in the appropriate boxes to change the toggle. The new setting will remain in effect until you specifically change it.
5. Click on OK to save the changes and exit.

Note: You can change all of the options at once.

Equations

Menu Bar: File (Preferences, Equations)

CUA Keyboard: <Ctrl><Shift><F1>

WordPerfect 5.1 Keyboard: Not Available

Description: Allows you to change the default keyboard, graphic font size, and alignment when using the Equation Editor.

WordPerfect
Defaults: *Keyboard:* Select

                       Graphic Font Size: Default Font

                       Horizontal Alignment: Center

                       Vertical Alignment: Center

                       Print as Graphics: On

Procedure: 1. Select the File Menu from anywhere in
                          WordPerfect.

                       2. Choose Preferences.

                       3. Choose Equations.

                       4. Click on the item you want to change and
                          use the up/down arrows to choose the
                          new default. If you want to change the de-
                          fault equation keyboard, clicking on Select
                          takes you to the Keyboard Preferences
                          Menu, allowing you to use any keyboard
                          in WordPerfect.

                       5. Click on OK to save the changes and exit
                          the menu.

See Also: *Equations* (Chapter 9); *Keyboard.*

Fast Save (Unformatted) _____

See *Environment.*

Format Retrieved Document for Default Printer ___

See *Display Preferences.*

Graphics Files Location _____

See *Location of Files.*

_____ *Graphics in Black and White*

See *Display Preferences.*

_____ *Hard Return Character*

See *Display Preferences.*

_____ *Hyphenation File Location*

See *Location of Files.*

_____ *Hyphenation Settings*

See *Environment.*

_____ *Initial Codes*

Menu Bar: File (Preferences, Initial Codes)

CUA Keyboard: <Ctrl><Shift><F1>

WordPerfect 5.1 Keyboard: Not Available

Description: Allows you to change the default formatting options established by WordPerfect when the application is accessed.

WordPerfect Default: Justification Left

Procedure:
1. Select the File Menu from anywhere in WordPerfect.
2. Choose Preferences.
3. Choose Initial Codes. You can now add codes to change the margins, create default

fonts, and the like. The codes will be in effect every time you create a document.

4. Click on Close to save the changes and
exit the screen. The new settings will be in
effect as the new default settings, remaining until specifically changed in this menu.
They can be overridden in each document
as formatting changes are made.

See Also: *Codes, Initial* (Chapter 3).

Keyboard

Menu Bar: File (Preferences, Keyboard)

CUA
Keyboard: <Ctrl><Shift><F1>

WordPerfect
5.1 Keyboard: Not Available

Description: Allows you to change from the CUA keyboard to the MS-DOS WordPerfect keyboard,
or to create your own keystroke assignments.

WordPerfect
Default: CUA Keyboard

Procedure: 1. Select the File Menu from anywhere in
WordPerfect.

2. Choose Preferences.

3. Choose Keyboard.

4. Click on Select to choose the MS-DOS
WordPerfect 5.1 keyboard or any other
keyboard on the pop-up list; click on Create to assign keystrokes to your own keyboard; click on Default to select the CUA
keyboard.

5. Click on OK to save the changes and exit
from the menu. The new keyboard layout

will remain in effect until you return to
this menu to change it.

See Also: Keyboard, Creating

Keyboard, Creating

Menu Bar: File (Preferences, Keyboard)

**CUA
Keyboard:**   <Ctrl><Shift><F1>

**WordPerfect
5.1 Keyboard:**   Not Available

Description: Allows you to assign keystrokes (representing
often used commands or scientific characters,
for example) to a keyboard.

Procedure: 1. Select the File Menu from anywhere in
WordPerfect.

2. Choose Preferences.

3. Choose Keyboard.

4. Click on Create.

5. Assignable items from the command,
menu, text, and macro directories are displayed on the left-hand side of the
screen. Click and drag to see the list of
assignable items for each category.

6. Highlight the assignable item that you
want to add. Its current keystroke assignment (if any) appears in the Keystrokes
Assigned to Item box.

7. In the Change Assignment box, enter a
keystroke or combination of keystrokes
that you want assigned to the assignable
item.

8. Click on Assign.

9. Repeat steps 5 through 8 to add other commands and menus to the new keyboard assignment list.

10. Click on OK to save the changes and go to the Save Keyboard File dialog box.

11. Enter a name for the new keyboard and click on Save to save the changes and return to the main Keyboard display.

12. The new keyboard is shown as the selected keyboard.

  a. Press OK to select the keyboard and return to your document.

  b. If you don't want to select the new keyboard now, click on Select to choose another keyboard. Then press OK to select the keyboard and return to your document.

Keyboards File Location

See *Location of Files.*

Language

Menu Bar:	Tools (Language)
Function Keys:	Not Available
Description:	Allows you to use a speller and thesaurus in a language other than American English if you have purchased the additional-language files from WordPerfect.
WordPerfect Default:	US

Procedure: 1. Select the Tools Menu at the point in your document that you need the alternate speller or thesaurus.

   2. Choose Language.

   3. Scroll through the language choices until you find the language that you want and highlight it, or click on Other to type in the two-letter code for the language.

   4. Click on OK to save the change and return to your document.

   5. Move the cursor to the point where the foreign-language speller/thesaurus is no longer needed.

   6. Select the Tools Menu.

   7. Choose Language.

   8. Click on US, returning the document to the default setting.

   9. Click on OK to save the change and exit the menu.

See Also: *Speller* (Chapter 6); *Thesaurus* (Chapter 6).

Location of Files

Menu Bar: File (Preferences, Location of Files)

CUA Keyboard: <Ctrl><Shift><F1>

WordPerfect 5.1 Keyboard: Not Available

Description: Allows you to change the location of your auxiliary files (backup, keyboard macros, graphics, main and supplemental dictionaries, printer files, hyphenation modules, spreadsheets, style library filename, and thesaurus).

WordPerfect Default:	The directory that includes your WordPerfect application files
Procedure:	1. Select the File Menu from anywhere in WordPerfect.
	2. Choose Preferences.
	3. Choose Location of Files.
	4. Use the mouse to move the cursor to the auxiliary file whose location you want to add or change.
	5. Type a complete pathname for new location, for example, b:\backup\<Enter>. The new setting will remain in effect until you specifically change it.
	6. Click on OK to save the changes and exit.
Notes:	1. The default directory for the supplemental speller dictionary is whatever you have chosen as your default directory for that session, unless you use the Location of Files to specify a different location.
	2. If you use Quick List, these changes will automatically be updated.

Macro Files Location

See *Location of Files.*

Merge

Menu Bar:	File (Preferences, Merge)
CUA Keyboard:	<Ctrl><Shift><F1>
WordPerfect 5.1 Keyboard:	Not Available

Description: Allows you to set Field and Record Delimiters to determine the beginning and end of each field and record in exported files.

**WordPerfect
Default:** None

Procedure:
1. Select the File Menu from anywhere in WordPerfect.
2. Choose Preferences.
3. Choose Merge.
4. Click on the arrow box of the item you want to define; drag the mouse to select Tab, Line Feed, Form Feed, or Carriage Return. The new settings will remain in effect until you specifically change them.
5. Click on OK to save the changes and exit the menu.

See Also: *Merge* (Chapter 8).

_____ *Menu Settings*

See *Environment*.

_____ *Numbers, Display and Entry of*

See *Display Preferences*.

_____ *Printer File Location*

See *Location of Files*.

_____ *Printer, Initial Settings*

Menu Bar: File (Preferences, Print)

CUA
Keyboard: <Ctrl><Shift><F1>

WordPerfect
5.1 Keyboard: Not Available

Description: Displays the default printer settings and allows them to be changed.

Table 2.4.   Printer Defaults

Printer Default Settings	
Number of Copies	1
Binding Offset	0″
Text Quality	High
Fast Graphics Printing	On
Generated By	WordPerfect
Graphics Quality	Medium
Redline Method	Printer Dependent

Size Attribute Ratios	
Fine	60%
Small	80%
Large	120%
Very Large	150%
Extra Large	200%
Super/Subscript	60%

Procedure: 1. Select the File Menu from anywhere in WordPerfect.

2. Choose Preferences.

3. Choose Print.

4. Click on the item you want to change.

5. Use the up and down arrow boxes to select a new value.

6. Click on OK to save the changes and leave the Preference Menu.

Notes: 1. You can change all items at once.

2. These settings are overridden by printer settings specifically added to a document.

See Also: *Font Attributes* (Chapter 5), *Printer Commands* (Chapter 11), *Redline Method* (Chapter 5).

_____ *Reveal Codes Colors*

Menu Bar: File (Preferences, Display, Reveal Codes Colors)

CUA
Keyboard: <Ctrl><Shift><F1>

WordPerfect
5.1 Keyboard: Not Available

Description: Allows you to change the Reveal Codes text, codes, and cursor color and background colors (within the limits of your monitor).

Procedure: 1. Select the File Menu from anywhere in WordPerfect.

2. Choose Preferences.

3. Choose Display.

4. Choose Reveal Codes Colors.

5. Click on the attribute you want to change.

6. Click on the foreground and/or background color whose appearance you want to change on the Reveal Codes screen. (You can click on Reset to return the screen to its original appearance.)

7. Click on OK to save the changes and exit.

See Also: *Reveal Codes* (Chapter 4).

Scroll Bar Settings ————————————————

See *Display Preferences*.

Speller File Location ————————————————

See *Location of Files*.

Spreadsheet File Location ———————————————

See *Location of Files*.

Status Bar Display Measurements ————————

See *Display Preferences*.

Styles File Location ————————————————

See *Location of Files*.

Table of Authorities ————————————————

Menu Bar:	File (Preferences, Table of Authorities)
CUA Keyboard:	\<Ctrl>\<Shift>\<F1>
WordPerfect 5.1 Keyboard:	Not Available
Description:	Allows you to change formatting items in the Table of Authorities.
WordPerfect Defaults:	*Dot Leaders:* On
	Underlining Allowed: Off
	Blank Line Between Authorities: On

Procedure: 1. Select the File Menu from anywhere in WordPerfect.

2. Choose Preferences.

3. Choose Table of Authorities.

4. Click on the box of the item you want to change. You can change all the items at once. The toggle switches will remain in effect until you specifically change them.

5. Click on OK to save the changes and exit the program.

See Also: *Table of Authorities* (Chapter 7).

_____ *Text in Windows Systems Color*

See *Display Preferences*.

_____ *Thesaurus File Location*

See *Location of Files*.

_____ *Ruler Settings*

See *Environment*.

_____ *Undo, Allow*

See *Environment*.

_____ *Units of Measure*

See *Display Preferences*.

3

Manipulating Files

This chapter describes the commands you will use as you work with files. These commands, unlike formatting commands, all involve physically changing a document; for example, renaming a file, deleting it, comparing a screen and disk document, and converting files from one format to another.

ANSI Text

See *Save As*.

ASCII Text

See *Save As*.

Assign Applications to Menu

See *File Manager Assign Applications to Menu*.

Button Bar

Menu Bar:	View (Button Bar Setup, Edit or New)
Function Keys:	Not Available
Description:	Allows you to put your most-used functions in one menu that you can name and place on the top, bottom, or side of your screen.

**WordPerfect
Default:**   On, Button Bar on Top

Procedure:
1. Select the View Menu.
2. Choose Button Bar Setup.
3. Choose Edit or New.
4. Click on the features that you want from the menus.
5. If you want to add a macro, click on Assign Macro to Button... to activate the Assign Macro to Button dialog box. Choose the desired macro (through the Macro Menu) and click on the Assign box.
6. Click on OK. If the Button Bar does not currently have a name, type in a name not exceeding eight characters. The new Button Bar is now active.

Notes:
1. If you do not want to use the Button Bar, click on Button Bar in the View Menu.
2. If you want the Button Bar on the side instead of on the top of the screen, select the Options box in the Button Bar Setup Menu.
3. If you want more than nine buttons on your Button Bar, use the Options Box to select Text Only, so that you can see all of the buttons at once.

See Also: Macros (Chapter 7).

Clear Screen _____

Menu Bar: Not Available

**CUA
Keyboard:**   ⟨Ctrl⟩⟨Shift⟩⟨F4⟩

WordPerfect 5.1 Keyboard:	\<Ctrl>\<Shift>\<F7>
Description:	Allows you to clear the screen of the current document.
Procedure:	1. Select Clear.
	2. A box appears asking "Discard Current Document?" Click on Yes to clear the screen, No to cancel the action.
Note:	WordPerfect does not ask if you want to save the document before the screen is cleared.
See Also:	*Save; Save As*.

Close a File

Menu Bar:	File (Close)
CUA Keyboard:	\<Ctrl>\<F4>
WordPerfect 5.1 Keyboard:	\<F7>
Description:	Allows you to close a file and clear the screen.
Procedure:	1. Select the File Menu.
	2. Choose Close. If no changes have been made to the file since it was last saved, the screen will clear. If changes have been made, a box prompts you to save the changes.

Codes, Initial

Menu Bar:	Layout (Document)

CUA
Keyboard: <Ctrl><Shift><F9>

WordPerfect
5.1 Keyboard: <Shift><F8>

Description: Allows you to set codes that will affect the entire document.

WordPerfect
Default: Left Justification

Procedure: 1. Select Layout on a blank screen or at the beginning of an existing document.

2. Choose Document.

3. Click on Initial Codes.

4. Set defaults for this document only (margins, tabs, justification, and the like).

5. Click on OK to save the changes and return to your document.

Compare Document _____

See *Document Compare*.

Convert from Other Format _____

Menu Bar: File (Open)

CUA
Keyboard: <F4>

WordPerfect
5.1 Keyboard: <Shift><F10>

Description: Allows you to bring documents into WordPerfect with different formats (Table 3.1, at the end of this command, contains a list of supported formats).

WordPerfect
Default: WordPerfect 5.1

Procedure: 1. Select File.

2. Choose Open.

3. Double-click on the document you want to retrieve.

4. WordPerfect asks you to confirm the document's format by clicking on OK or using the scroll bar to highlight the current format.

5. WordPerfect makes the conversion, opening the file.

Note: If you have a number of files to convert, you can use the Convert.exe utility that shipped with your MS-DOS WordPerfect 5.1 program, or you can call WordPerfect to purchase the Convert utility separately.

Table 3.1. WordPerfect Conversion Formats

Available Formats	Versions Supported
Ami Pro	1.2, 1.2a, 1.2b
ANSI (Windows)	Delimited Text, Generic Word Processor
ASCII (DOS)	Delimited Text, Generic Word Processor, Text
DisplayWrite	4.0, 4.2, 5.0
IBM	DCA/FFT, DCA/RFT
MS Word	5.0, 5.5
MS Word for Windows	1.0, 1.1, 1.1a
MultiMate	3.3, 3.6, Advantage II (3.7), 4.0
OfficeWriter	6.0, 6.1, 6.11, 6.2
Rich Text Format	
WordPerfect	4.2, 5.0, 5.1
WordStar	3.3, 3.31, 3.4, 4.0, 5.0, 5.5, 6.0
XyWrite	III Plus, 3.55, 3.56

Note:	WordPerfect assumes a text file is ASCII if all the characters in the file are from the ASCII character set. If you want the file converted as an ANSI text file, be sure to specify that format when prompted.
See Also:	*Save As*.

Copy File

Menu Bar:	File (Open, Options)
CUA Keyboard:	\<F4\>
Function Keys:	\<Shift\>\<F10\>
Description:	Allows you to copy a file on disk to another disk (hard or floppy).
Procedure:	1. Select File from anywhere in WordPerfect.
	2. Double-click on the directory where the document is located.
	3. Highlight the document to be copied.
	4. Choose Options/Copy.
	5. Enter the complete pathname of the destination directory (i.e., C:\word\files or A:\).
	6. Click on Copy.
Notes:	1. If you have several files to copy to the same place, use the File Manager.
	2. If the file to be copied is open (on your screen), use the Save As command rather than the Copy file command. The Copy File command copies the file that was last written to the directory, and it may not be the most current.

3. If the file you are copying already exists in the destination directory, WordPerfect will ask if you want to overwrite the file in that directory. Be sure of which file you want to keep before you tell WordPerfect Yes.

See Also: *File Manager Copy File; Save As.*

_____ *Create Directory*

See *File Manager Create Directory.*

_____ *Default Mode*

See *Draft Mode.*

_____ *Delete Files*

Menu Bar:	File (Open, Options)
CUA Keyboard:	\<F4\>
Function Keys:	\<Shift\>\<F10\>
Description:	Allows you to delete a file on disk.
Procedure:	1. Select File anywhere in WordPerfect.
	2. Double-click on the desired directory.
	3. Highlight the document.
	4. Click on Options.
	5. Click on Delete.
Notes:	1. If you have several files to be deleted from the same directory, use the File Manager program. Alternatively, if the files have the same extension (.abc, for example), you

can enter a wildcard pattern to delete them.

2. If the file you want to delete is open (on your screen), do not save it after deleting it from the directory.

See Also: *File Manager Delete Files; Cut* (Chapter 4).

Document Comments _____

Menu Bar: Tools (Comment)

**Function
Keys:**   Not Available

Description: Allows you to place a comment inside the text. The comment will be displayed but it will never be printed unless you convert it to text.

Procedure: 1. Select the Tools Menu.

2. Choose Comment.

3. Choose Create.

4. Type your comment.

5. Add any font attributes you want.

6. Click on OK to return to your document. The comment is now displayed.

Note: If you are editing or converting your comment, position the cursor to the right of the comment before you start. WordPerfect works backward to the first comment it finds.

Document Compare _____

Menu Bar: Tools (Document Compare)

Function Keys:	Not Available
Description:	Allows you to compare a document on the screen with the previously saved document on disk.
Procedure:	1. Select Tools.
	2. Choose Document Compare.
	3. Choose Add Markings.
	4. Click on Compare to accept the default file choice, or type in the complete pathname and file title.
	5. The changes in the document on the screen are marked with redline (additions) and strikeout (deletions).
	6. To return to the original screen document, select Tools/Document Compare/Remove Markings. Click on OK to remove the redline and strikeout markings. Click on the box to retain the redline markings and remove the strikeout markings.
Notes:	1. If you want to retain the document on disk, save the screen file to a different filename.
	2. If you want to retain the additions or comments in the screen document but you do not want the redline or strikeout, search for and delete the redline and strikeout codes.
See Also:	*Redline/Strikeout* (Chapter 5); *Search* (Chapter 6).

_____ *Document Summary*

Menu Bar:	Layout (Document)

CUA
Keyboard: <Ctrl><Shift><F9>

WordPerfect
5.1 Keyboard: <Shift><F8>

Description: Allows you to create or edit a summary that helps locate files in later searches.

Procedure: 1. Select Layout from anywhere in your document.

                   2. Choose Document.

                   3. Choose Summary.

                   4. Click on the box of the item you wish to add or edit and enter the information.

                   5. If necessary, click on another box and add to or edit the information there.

                   6. Click on OK to save the changes and return to your document.

See Also: *Document Summary, Default* (Chapter 2).

Draft Mode

Menu Bar: View (Draft Mode)

Function
Keys: <Ctrl><Shift><F3>

Description: Allows you to work more easily with text than when you are in the Default Mode. Use the Default Mode when you are through working with text and are ready to format your document.

WordPerfect
Default: Default Mode

Procedure: 1. Select View at any point in your document.

2. Click on Draft Mode. The screen will change colors, and you will have a close-up view of the type you are using. Draft Mode/Default Mode is a toggle. To change back to Draft Mode, select Layout/Draft Mode again.

See Also: *Draft Mode Colors* (Chapter 2).

_____ *Exit WordPerfect*

Menu Bar:	File (Exit)
CUA Keyboard:	⟨Alt⟩⟨F4⟩
WordPerfect 5.1 Keyboard:	⟨F7⟩
Description:	Allows you to exit from WordPerfect.
Procedure:	1. Select the File Menu.
	2. Choose Exit. If no changes have been made to the file since it was last saved, you will be returned to the Windows Program Manager. If changes have been made, a box prompts you to save the changes before leaving the file and application.
Shortcut:	Double-click on the Control Menu icon (extreme upper left-hand corner).

_____ *File Attributes, Changing*

See *File Manager Attributes*.

File Manager Assign Applications to Menu _____

Menu Bar: File (File Manager, Applications)

**CUA
Keyboard:**   Not Available

**WordPerfect
5.1 Keyboard:**   <F5> (Applications)

Description: Allows you to assign applications to the
WordPerfect File Manager.

Procedure:
1. Select File at any point in your document.
2. Choose File Manager.
3. Select the Applications Menu Bar.
4. Click on Assign to Menu.
5. A list of the current applications assigned
   to the Applications Menu Bar appears.
   Click on the Scroll Bar icon at the end of
   the command line to add an application
   from the current directory or to change to
   the directory where the application is located.
6. Double-click on the application you want
   to add. It now appears in the list of current
   applications assigned to the Applications
   Menu Bar.
7. Click on OK to save your changes and return to the File Manager window.
8. Select File/Exit File Manager (or double-
   click on the Control Menu icon at the top
   left) to leave the File Manager and return
   to your document.

File Manager Associate _____

Menu Bar: File (File Manager)

**CUA
Keyboard:** Not Available

**WordPerfect
5.1 Keyboard:** ⟨F5⟩

Description: Allows you to associate a non-WordPerfect application with a file and type or a file extension.

Procedure: 1. Select File at any point in your document.

2. Choose File Manager.

3. Select File.

4. Choose Preferences.

5. Click on Associate.

6. A dialog box will appear that lists the available file types and extensions. Scroll through them and highlight the entries you want to change. When you have finished, click on Change to confirm the changes, then click on Close to return to the File Manager.

7. Click on File/Exit File Manager to leave the File Manager window, or double-click on the Control Menu icon (extreme upper left-hand corner).

File Manager Attributes

Menu Bar: File (File Manager, File)

**CUA
Keyboard:** Not Available

**WordPerfect
5.1 Keyboard:** ⟨F5⟩ (File)

Description: Allows you to change properties of specified files: read only, hidden, archive, or systems.

WordPerfect Default:	Off
Procedure:	1. Select File at any point in your document.
	2. Choose File Manager.
	3. Select File or press <Ctrl>A.
	4. Choose Change Attributes.
	5. A dialog box appears. Click on the property you want to change.
	6. Click on Change to change the file attributes and return to the File Manager.
	7. Select File/Exit File Manager (or double-click on the Control Menu icon at the top left) to leave the File Manager and return to your document.

File Manager Copy File _____

Menu Bar:	File (File Manager, File)
CUA Keyboard:	Not Available
WordPerfect 5.1 Keyboard:	<F5> (File)
Description:	Allows you to copy multiple files from one directory to another.
Procedure:	1. Select File at any point in your document.
	2. Choose File Manager.
	3. In Navigator, which is open unless you changed the default, click on the directory where the files are currently located.
	4. Select the files that you want copied from the directory. If you want to select all the files in the directory, highlight a file in the

directory, then select the Edit/Select All Menu Bar option.

5. Click on the Copy Button Bar icon or press <Ctrl>C.

6. A dialog box appears that prompts you for the pathname of the directory where you want the files copied. Enter the appropriate information. The files will be copied, with WordPerfect telling you the status of the copy.

7. When WordPerfect is through, click on OK to return to the File Manager.

8. Select File/Exit File Manager (or double-click on the Control Menu icon at the top left) to leave the File Manager and return to your document.

Note: If you have only one or two files to copy, use the File/Open/Options Menu to access the Copy command.

See Also: *Copy File*.

_____ *File Manager Create Directory*

Menu Bar: File (File Manager, File)

**CUA
Keyboard:**   Not Available

**WordPerfect
5.1 Keyboard:**   <F5> (<Ctrl>T)

Description: Allows you to create a new subdirectory.

Procedure: 1. Select File at any point in your document.

2. Choose File Manager.

3. In Navigator, which is open unless you changed the default, highlight a file in the

directory where you want to add a subdirectory.

4. Select File/Create Directory or press
   <Ctrl>T.

5. Enter the subdirectory name.

6. Select File/Exit File Manager (or double-
   click on the Control Menu icon at the top
   left) to leave the File Manager and return
   to your document.

File Manager Delete Files

Menu Bar:	File (File Manager, File)
CUA Keyboard:	Not Available
WordPerfect 5.1 Keyboard:	<F5> (File)
Description:	Allows you to delete multiple files at the same time.
Procedure:	1. Select File at any point in your document.

2. Choose File Manager.

3. In Navigator, which is open unless you
   changed the default, click on the directory
   where the files are currently located.

4. Select the files in the directory that you
   want deleted. If you want to select all the
   files in the directory, highlight a file in the
   directory, then select the Edit/Select All
   Menu Bar option.

5. Click on the Delete Button Bar icon or
   press <Ctrl>D.

6. A dialog box appears that lists the files to
   be deleted. Click on the appropriate delete
   box to delete all the listed files or selected

files. The files will be deleted, with Word-Perfect telling you the status of the process.

7. Select File/Exit File Manager (or double-click on the Control Menu icon at the top left) to leave the File Manager and return to your document.

Note: If you have only one or two files to delete and you are currently in WordPerfect, not the File Manager, use the File/Open/Options Menu to access the Delete command.

See Also: *Delete Files*.

_____ *File Manager Information*

Menu Bar: File (File Manager)

**CUA
Keyboard:**   Not Available

**WordPerfect
5.1 Keyboard:**   <F5>

Description: Allows you to review information about your system, Windows, available printers, and your disks. It also allows this information to be printed.

Procedure: 1. Select File at any point in your document.
2. Choose File Manager.
3. Select Info.
4. Click on the topic you need to know about.
5. A dialog box will appear that gives you information about the topic. Click on OK to exit the topic and return to the File Manager window.

6. If you want the information printed, select Info.

   a. Click on Print Info Report.

   b. If you do not want all the topics printed, click on their boxes to turn them off. The default is to include all the topics in the Info Report.

   c. Click on OK to print the Info Report and return to the File Manager screen.

7. Select File/Exit File Manager (or double-click on the Control Menu icon at the top left) to leave the File Manager and return to your document.

File Manager List Files

Menu Bar: File (File Manager)

**CUA
Keyboard:**   Not Available

**WordPerfect
5.1 Keyboard:**   ⟨F5⟩

Description: Allows you to look at the files in a specified directory.

Procedure: 1. Select File at any point in your document.

2. Choose File Manager.

3. Select View or press ⟨Ctrl⟩F.

4. Click on File List. The files in the default subdirectory will appear.

5. To change the default directory, enter a new directory in the directory dialog box or double-click on the [...] box in the File List window.

Note: If you are only interested in one directory and you are not currently in the File Manager, use the File/Open Menu to list all the files. If you are currently in the File Manager, the Navigator can list all the files, too, only faster, allowing you to see the root structure as you go.

See Also: *File Manager Navigator; Open a File.*

_____ *File Manager Move/Rename*

Menu Bar: File (File Manager, File)

**CUA
Keyboard:**   Not Available

**WordPerfect
5.1 Keyboard:**   <F5> (<Ctrl>R)

Description: Allows you to move multiple files from one directory to another.

Procedure: 1. Select File at any point in your document.

2. Choose File Manager.

3. In Navigator, which is open unless you changed the default, click on the directory where the files are currently located.

4. Select the files in the directory that you want moved. If you want to select all the files in the directory, highlight a file in the directory, then select the Edit/Select All Menu Bar option.

5. Click on the Move Button Bar icon, or press <Ctrl>R.

6. A dialog box appears that prompts you for the pathname of the directory to which you want the files moved. Enter the appropriate information. The files will be transferred, with WordPerfect telling you the

status of the move. The files are deleted from the source directory.

7. When WordPerfect is through, click on OK to return to the File Manager.

8. Select File/Exit File Manager (or double-click on the Control Menu icon at the top left) to leave the File Manager and return to your document.

Note: If you want to rename a file, highlight it and press <Ctrl>R. The same screen will appear. Give the file its new name; if you do not specify a different directory, the file will be saved under its new name in the same directory. The original file will be deleted. This command can also be accessed from the File/Open/Options Menu.

File Manager Navigator

Menu Bar: File (File Manager)

**CUA
Keyboard:** Not Available

**WordPerfect
5.1 Keyboard:** <F5>

Description: Allows you to see and manipulate all the files in your system.

Procedure:
1. Select File at any point in your document.

2. Choose File Manager.

3. The File Manager window appears; if you have not changed the default, the Navigator is at the top of the screen.

4. To see any file on your system, click on the root directory where the file is located, then click on each succeeding subdirectory

until you get to the file or subdirectory in question.

5. At this point, you can view, copy, delete, move, or print any highlighted file. (To highlight more than one file, use the mouse to click and drag.)

6. When you have finished manipulating the files, leave the File Manager by selecting File/Exit File Manager or double-clicking on the Control Menu icon at the upper left-hand corner.

See Also: *File Manager Copy File; File Manager Delete File; File Manager Move/Rename; File Manager Print; File Manager Viewer.*

File Manager Print

Menu Bar: File (File Manager)

CUA Keyboard: Not Available

WordPerfect 5.1 Keyboard: <F5>(<Ctrl>P)

Description: Allows you to print the files that you are manipulating in File Manager. You can also use File Manager to print multiple WordPerfect files without opening them.

Procedure:
1. Choose File at any point in your document.

2. Choose File Manager.

3. Use the Navigator to go to the directory where you want a file or files printed.

4. Use the mouse to highlight the files you want printed.

        5. Click on File/Print to print the document(s).

        6. A dialog box will appear, prompting you to Print or Cancel. Click on Print to print the file(s). You will automatically be returned to your document.

Note: WordPerfect is not a multitasking application. You will not be able to work on anything else until all of the jobs have been sent to the printer.

See Also: *File Manager Navigator*.

File Manager Print Window

Menu Bar: File (File Manager)

CUA
Keyboard: Not Available

WordPerfect
5.1 Keyboard: ⟨F5⟩

Description: Allows you to print the contents of any Navigator window without selecting all the files in the window.

Procedure: 1. Select File at any point in your document.

        2. Choose File Manager.

        3. In Navigator, which should be open unless you changed the default, click on the subdirectories until you open the one whose contents you want printed.

        4. Click on any file in the subdirectory.

        5. Select File.

        6. Click on Print Window.

        7. A dialog box will appear, giving you the option of printing the entire list or only se-

lected files. Printing the entire list is the default.

8. Click on OK to print the window and return to the File Manager.

9. Use the File/Exit File Manager menu to return to your document, or double-click on the Control Menu icon in the upper left-hand corner.

See Also: *File Manager Navigator*.

File Manager Search

Menu Bar: File (File Manager)

CUA Keyboard: Not Available

WordPerfect 5.1 Keyboard: <F5>

Description: Allows you to look for specific words and files.

Table 3.2. Advanced Find Defaults

Advanced Find Attributes	Default
Apply Find to	Current Window
Limit Find to	Document Text
Find Method	Word Search
Find Multiple Words in	Same File

Procedure:
1. Select File at any point in your document.

2. Choose File Manager.

3. In Navigator, which should be open unless you changed the default, click on the subdirectories until you open the one whose contents you want to search.

4. Select Search.

  5. Click on Find Words, Find Files, or Advanced Find, depending on how sophisticated a search you are doing.

  6. Enter the word pattern you want.

  7. Click on Find.

  8. The search will take place. Files that match the search criteria will appear in a list, which you can then manipulate as needed.

  9. Use the File/Exit File Manager menu to return to your document, or double-click on the Control Menu icon in the upper left-hand corner.

Note: If you just want to search for files or words in one directory, use the File/Open/Options Menu to access the Find function.

See Also: *Find a File; Search* (Chapter 6).

File Manager View Layout _____

Menu Bar: File (File Manager)

**CUA
Keyboard:** Not Available

**WordPerfect
5.1 Keyboard:** <F5>

Description: Allows you to change the File Manager window layout.

Procedure:
  1. Select File at any point in your document.
  2. Choose File Manager.
  3. Select View.
  4. Click on Layout.
  5. A number of options appear; choose the one that is most appropriate. Wide Navigator, Viewer is the default.

6. Use the File/Exit File Manager menu to re-turn to your document, or double-click on the Control Menu icon in the upper left-hand corner.

File Manager Viewer

Menu Bar:	File (File Manager)
CUA Keyboard:	Not Available
WordPerfect 5.1 Keyboard:	⟨F5⟩
Description:	Allows you to view the files highlighted in the Navigator.
Procedure:	1. Select File at any point in your document.
	2. Choose File Manager.
	3. Viewer should be on the bottom of your screen if you have not changed the default.
	4. When you highlight a file (not a subdirectory), the file appears in the Viewer window.
	5. When you have finished with File Manager, use the File/Exit File Manager Menu to return to your document, or double-click on the Control Menu icon in the upper left-hand corner.
Note:	You do not need this command if you are working exclusively in WordPerfect. You can see files before opening them through the File/Open/View Menu.
See Also:	*File Manager View Layout; Open a File; View*.

Find a File _____

Menu Bar:	File (Open, Options)
CUA Keyboard:	\<F4\>
WordPerfect 5.1 Keyboard:	\<Shift\>\<F10\>
Description:	Allows you to locate a copy of a file on disk.
Procedure:	1. Select File from anywhere in WordPerfect.
	2. Choose Open.
	3. Choose Options.
	4. Click on Find.
	4. Enter the search criteria (pattern to search for) and indicate whether you want the search confined to the subdirectory, the root directory, or the whole drive.
	5. Click on Find Files or Find Words.
	6. When the appropriate file is found, you can use the Options box to move/rename the file, copy it, or delete it. You can also view it in this window.
Note:	You can also use this command through the File Manager/Search/Find Words or Find Files Menu Bar.

Import DDE Documents _____

See *DDE Link* (Chapter 10).

Import Spreadsheets _____

See **Chapter 10**.

Import Word Processing Applications

See _Convert from Other Format_.

List Files

See _File Manager List Files_.

Locked Documents

See _Password_.

Master Document

See **Chapter 7**.

Move/Rename File

Menu Bar:	File (Open, Options)
CUA Keyboard:	⟨F4⟩
WordPerfect 5.1 Keyboard:	⟨Shift⟩⟨F10⟩
Description:	Allows you to move or rename a file on disk.
WordPerfect Default:	Default Directory
Procedure:	1. Select File from anywhere in WordPerfect.
	2. Choose Open.
	3. Highlight the document to be moved or re-named.
	4. Choose Options.

5. Click on Move/Rename.

6. Enter the complete pathname of the destination directory (i.e., C:\word\files or A:\).
If you want the file to have a new name,
enter that along with the pathname. If you
want the file to remain in the same directory with the new name, just change the
name and leave the directory as the default.

7. Click on Move.

Notes:
1. If you have several files to move to the
same place, use the File Manager.

2. If the file to be moved is open (on your
screen), use the Save As command rather
than the Move/Rename command. The
Move/Rename command moves the file
that was last written to the directory,
which may not be the most current.

3. If the file you are moving already exists in
the destination directory, WordPerfect will
ask if you want to overwrite the file in that
directory. Be sure of which file you want
to keep before you tell WordPerfect Yes.

4. Do not rename (or move to another directory) files that are being used in desktop
publishing applications, such as Ventura
Publisher, because desktop publishing files
frequently generate other files, using the
original filename as a reference. A desktop
publishing file whose name is changed is a
file that cannot be found or loaded by the
desktop publishing application.

See Also: *File Manager Move/Rename* to move multiple files at once; *Save As.*

Open a File

Menu Bar:	File (Open)
CUA Keyboard:	<F4>
WordPerfect 5.1 Keyboard:	<Shift><F10>
Description:	Allows you to open already-created files.
Procedure:	1. Select the File Menu.
	2. Choose Open.
	3. You are in the wpwin directory. To change directories, double-click on the [..] icon in the right-hand box, which will take you to the parent directory and show you all the subdirectories in that root directory. (If the box does not contain the [..] icon, click on the Quick List box at the bottom of the screen.)
	4. Double-click on the desired subdirectory. The files in that directory will appear in the left-hand box.
	5. Double-click on the desired file.
Shortcut:	At the bottom of the File Menu are the last four files you saved. Click on any of them instead of retrieving the file from the directory.
See Also:	*Draft Mode; Quick List*.

Password

Menu Bar:	File (Password)
Function Keys:	Not Available

Description: Allows you to put a password on specified documents so that anyone who does not have the code is prevented from retrieving a locked file.

WordPerfect
Default: Off

Procedure:
1. Select File from anywhere in your document.

2. Choose Password.

3. Enter the password for the document and click on Set.

4. At the prompt, retype your password and click on Set again. Password protection takes effect as soon as you save your document.

Notes:
1. To remove password protection, retrieve the document, return to the File/Password Menu, and select Remove.

2. Once you have added a password to a file, you must use the password each time you want to retrieve the file. If you forget the password, you cannot ever retrieve the file and WordPerfect will not unlock it for you.

3. If you have password protection on a file and save the document as an ASCII or generic file or in an earlier version of WordPerfect, the password protection is lost.

4. Before you export your documents to desktop publishing packages, such as Ventura Publisher, remove the password protection. Otherwise, your document appears as a small amount of undecipherable garbage.

Quick List

Menu Bar:	File (Open)
CUA Keyboard:	<F4>
WordPerfect 5.1 Keyboard:	<Shift><F10>
Description:	Allows you to put your most frequently used directories and files in a special list for faster retrieval.
Procedure:	1. Select File.
	2. Choose Open.
	3. Click on the Quick List box.
	4. Click on Edit Quick List.
	5. Click on Add.
	6. Enter the complete pathname of the directory or file you wish to add to the Quick List (for example, c:\word or c:\word\letter.910). You can add a descriptive name if you like. The descriptive name is what you will see on the Quick List. The default is the full pathname.
Note:	You can also modify the Quick List while in the File Manager through the View menu.

Retrieve File

Menu Bar:	File (Retrieve)
Function Keys:	Not Available
Description:	Allows you to retrieve a file into the current document.

Procedure:	1. Select File at the point in your document where you want the new file to begin.
	2. Choose Retrieve. This takes you to the default directory.
	3. Double-click on the file to be retrieved, or type the complete pathname of the desired document and click on Retrieve.
	4. A box will appear, asking if you want the file inserted into the current document. Click on Yes.
Notes:	1. Be sure that the cursor is positioned where you want the new document to start.
	2. You can also use the Retrieve option through the File Manager.
See Also:	*DDE Link* (Chapter 10), to import files from Windows applications into a WordPerfect document.
	Spreadsheet, Import (Chapter 10), to import spreadsheet data into a WordPerfect document.

Save _____

Menu Bar:	File (Save)
CUA Keyboard:	<Shift><F3>
WordPerfect 5.1 Keyboard:	<F10>
Description:	Allows you to save a file.

Procedure: 1. Select the File Menu.

2. Choose Save. If the file has never been saved, a menu box will prompt you to give the file an 11-character name, including the extension. If the file already has a name, it will be automatically saved.

Notes: 1. To save a file to another directory, with another name, or in a different format, use the Save As command.

2. Do not use the Timed Backup feature in place of a formal save. Timed Backup files are deleted when you exit properly from WordPerfect. In addition, the Timed Backup feature does not distinguish between the file you are working on now and the file you worked on 15 minutes ago; the latest Timed Backup for each window overwrites all previous Timed Backup files for that window.

See Also: *Save As*.

_____ *Save As*

Menu Bar: File (Save As)

CUA Keyboard: <F3>

WordPerfect 5.1 Keyboard: <F10>

Description: Allows you to save a file with a different name or in a different format.

Procedure: 1. Select File from anywhere in the document that you want saved. (The document must be on the screen to use the Save As feature.)

2. Choose Save As.

   a. To rename the document, enter the complete pathname and document name and click on Save.

   b. To save the document to a different format, use the Format scroll bar to locate the format you want. Then enter the complete pathname and document name and click on Save.

See Also: *Convert from Different Format*, for a list of supported word processor types.

Save File to Earlier WordPerfect Version ⎯⎯⎯⎯⎯⎯⎯⎯⎯⎯⎯⎯⎯⎯⎯

See *Save As*.

View ⎯⎯⎯⎯⎯⎯⎯⎯⎯⎯⎯⎯⎯⎯⎯⎯⎯⎯⎯⎯⎯⎯⎯⎯⎯⎯⎯⎯⎯⎯

Menu Bar: File (Open, View)

Function Keys: Not Available

Description: Allows you to look at a file in formatted form before you retrieve it to the screen.

Procedure:
1. Select File at any point in WordPerfect.
2. Choose Open.
3. Highlight a file.
4. Click on View. The highlighted file now appears in a box in the upper right-hand corner. You can see it as it will appear on your Default Mode screen, and you can maneuver through it by clicking on the View Window and then using the arrow keys and mouse.

5. To view another file, highlight it. The new file will take the place of the old file in the View Window.

6. To retrieve a document that is in the View Window, click on Open.

See Also: *Print Preview* (Chapter 11) to view a document before you print it.

_____ *Word Processing Applications, Saving to*

See *Save As*.

4

Manipulating the Page

This chapter deals with the commands and features that affect the page and the text on the page: commands such as cutting and pasting, adding headers or footers and endnotes or footnotes, and preventing text from standing alone at the bottom or top of a page.

Append

Menu Bar:	Edit (Append)
Function Keys:	Not Available
Description:	Allows you to add text or graphics to the end of the Clipboard.
Procedure:	1. Block the text to be appended.
	2. Select the Edit Menu.
	3. Click on Append.
Note:	The text will not be deleted from the current file when it is added to the Clipboard. You must delete it specifically from the current text.
See Also:	*Clipboard* (Appendix A).

Block Protect

Menu Bar:	Layout (Page, Block Protect)

**CUA
Keyboard:**   <Alt><F9>

**WordPerfect
5.1 Keyboard:** <Shift><F8>

Description: Allows you to keep text within a set of codes
together on the same page.

**WordPerfect
Default:**   Off

Procedure: 1. Block the text you want protected.

2. Select Layout.

3. Choose Page.

4. Click on Block Protect. The block of text
will now be kept together on the same
page.

See Also: *Conditional End of Page; Page Break* (Chapter 5); *Widow/Orphan.*

Cancel _____

Menu Bar: Not Available

**CUA
Keyboard:**   <Esc>

**WordPerfect
5.1 Keyboard:** <F1>

Description: Allows you to "escape" from a menu or
dialog box, or to reverse your most recent action (restore deleted text, for example).

Clipboard _____

See *Clipboard* (**Appendix A**).

_____ *Codes*

See *Deleting Codes; Reveal Codes*.

_____ *Conditional End of Page*

Menu Bar: Layout (Page, Conditional End of Page)

**CUA
Keyboard:**   <Alt><F9>

**WordPerfect
5.1 Keyboard:**   <Shift><F8>

Description: Allows you to keep a specified number of
                   lines of text from being split by a page break.

**WordPerfect
Default:**   Off

Procedure: 1. Select Layout at the line above the lines
                      you want kept together.
                   2. Choose Page.
                   3. Click on Conditional End of Page.
                   4. Enter the number of lines you want kept
                      together.
                   5. Click on OK to save the changes and re-
                      turn to your document.

See Also: *Block Protect; Widow/Orphan*.

_____ *Cut*

Menu Bar: Edit (Cut)

**CUA
Keyboard:**   Select, <Shift><Delete>, or <Ctrl>X

**WordPerfect
5.1 Keyboard:**   Block, <Ctrl><F4>, or <Ctrl>X

Description: Allows you to delete text and graphics from the current document.

Procedure:
1. Select the text to be cut.
2. Press <Ctrl>X or select the Edit (Cut) Menu.
3. If you want to move the cut text else-where, move the cursor to the new location and press <Shift><Insert> (on the CUA Keyboard) or <F1> (on the WordPerfect 5.1 Keyboard).

Note: You can reverse the cut action with the Undelete or Undo keys; you cannot reverse the action with the <Esc> key.

Shortcuts:
1. Selecting text and using the <Delete> key (not <Shift><Delete>) to cut text is faster, as long as you do not want to retrieve the text again.
2. You can delete a word without blocking it: Position the cursor at the word and press <Ctrl> and ← simultaneously.

Date, Automatically Inserting _____

Menu Bar: Tools (Date)

CUA Keyboard: <Ctrl><Shift><F5>(Date Code)

WordPerfect 5.1 Keyboard: <Shift><F5>

Description: Allows you to insert either today's date into your document or a code that shows the current date whenever the document is retrieved.

Procedure:
1. Select Tools at the point in the document that you want the date printed.

2. Choose Date Text (if you want today's date) or Date Code (if you want the document printed with the current date every time). Choose Format to change the date format for this document only.

See Also: *Date, Format* (Chapter 2); *Merge* (Chapter 8).

_____ *Deleting Codes*

Menu Bar: View (Reveal Codes)

Function Keys: <Alt><F3>

Description: Allows you to check and eliminate formatting codes.

WordPerfect Default: Off

Procedure:
1. Select Reveal Codes at the point in the document you want to check.
2. Highlight the code you want to delete by moving the cursor to it.
3. Press <Delete>.
4. Press <Alt><F3> again to leave Reveal Codes.

Notes:
1. If you made a mistake deleting a formatting code, you can use the Cancel key (<Esc> or <F1>) to restore the code.
2. You can delete codes without being in Reveal Codes; WordPerfect will ask if you really mean to delete the code. If you are deleting text while you are in Reveal Codes, WordPerfect will delete the codes without asking.

3. Check Reveal Codes whenever your document does not behave properly. Extra formatting codes can cause your document to print improperly, move headers and footers from their specified locations, cause margins to move, and fonts to be completely ignored.

See Also: *Reveal Codes* (Chapter 1) for a discussion of concepts, and *Reveal Codes, Using*.

Delete Block of Text

See *Cut*.

Document Summary

Menu Bar: Layout (Document, Summary)

CUA Keyboard: <Ctrl><Shift><F9>

WordPerfect 5.1 Keyboard: <Shift><F8>

Description: Allows you to enter document information that will help in later searches.

Procedure:
1. Select Layout at any point in your document.
2. Choose Document.
3. Click on Summary.
4. Enter as much information as you want to provide. Use the <Tab> key to navigate among the boxes.
5. Click on OK to save the changes and return to your document.

Endnotes

See *Footnotes/Endnotes*.

Enter

Menu Bar:	Not Available
Function Keys:	⟨Enter⟩
Description:	Allows you to insert hard returns (extra line spaces) in your document. Hard returns do not move, unlike the soft returns that Word-Perfect inserts at the end of each line. (Soft returns disappear if you reformat your document; they reappear at the new end of lines.) WordPerfect cannot reformat hard returns.
See Also:	*Page Break* (Chapter 5).

Envelopes

Menu Bar:	Layout (Page, Paper Size)
CUA Keyboard:	⟨Alt⟩⟨F9⟩
WordPerfect 5.1 Keyboard:	⟨Shift⟩⟨F8⟩
Description:	Allows you to select a different paper size for envelopes.
Procedure:	1. Select Layout at top of the page where you want a different paper size.
	2. Choose Page.
	3. Click on Paper Size.

4. Highlight the appropriate paper definition.
Click on Select.

Note: Your document will now have new default margins forced by the new paper size from this point forward.

See Also: *Labels* (Chapter 8); *Paper Size* to create a new envelope definition.

Footers _____

See *Headers/Footers*.

Footnotes/Endnotes _____

Menu Bar: Layout (Footnote or Endnote)

**CUA
Keyboard:** Not Available

**WordPerfect
5.1 Keyboard:** <Ctrl><F7>

Description: Allows you to create footnotes and endnotes. WordPerfect automatically generates the correct footnote or endnote number, or it allows you to select your own.

Procedure for Creating a Footnote or Endnote:

1. Select Layout at the point in your document where you want the footnote/endnote number inserted.

2. Choose Footnote or Endnote.

3. Choose Options to select the style of your footnote/endnote. Make any necessary changes.

4. Click on OK to save the changes and return to your document.

5. Select Layout and Footnote or Endnote.

6. Choose Create.

7. Type the text of the footnote/endnote.

8. Click on Close to save your footnote/endnote and return to your document.

Procedure for Editing a Footnote or Endnote:

1. Select Layout at any point in your document.

2. Choose Footnote or Endnote.

3. Choose Edit.

4. Choose the number of the footnote/endnote you want to edit, or click on OK to accept the default (which is the closest number, going backwards, to your present cursor location).

5. Edit your footnote/endnote.

6. Click on OK to save the changes and return to your document.

Procedure for Changing a Footnote or Endnote Number:

1. Select Layout.

2. When the cursor is to the left of the footnote/endnote number, choose Footnote or Endnote.

3. Choose New Number.

4. Type the new number or accept the default.

5. Click on OK to save the changes and return to the screen. The footnotes/endnotes are now automatically renumbered from this point in the document forward.

Procedure for Deleting a Footnote or Endnote:

1. Move the cursor to the footnote/endnote number.

2. Press <Backspace> or <Delete> to delete the number. This automatically deletes the footnote/endnote as well.

Procedure for Endnote Placement Code:

If you want the endnotes to print somewhere other than the end of the file, you must insert a endnote placement code at the point in your document where you want the endnotes printed.

1. Select Layout and Endnote at the point in your document where you want a endnote placement code, and create a page break (<Ctrl><Enter>).

2. Choose Endnote Placement.

3. Click on Yes if you want endnotes after the endnote placement code to use a different numbering sequence than the endnotes before the endnote placement code. Click on No if you want endnotes following the endnote placement code to continue with the established numbering sequence.

4. To determine how much space the endnotes will take up, select Tools (Generate).

5. Click on OK to generate the endnotes. The Endnote Placement Message that appears takes up the actual amount of space the endnotes will use when printed. It is followed by a page break.

Notes:

1. Footnotes and endnotes are not related to headers and footers, which provide repeating information (such as a page number and chapter title) on each page.

2. Footnotes and endnotes do not appear in their entirety on the screen. (The first 50 characters do show up in Reveal Codes.) The only ways to view created footnotes

and endnotes are to return to the footnote
edit screen or to use the Print Preview feature (File, Print Preview).

3. Do not attempt to center a page top to bottom if the page has endnotes or footnotes
on it.

See Also: *Headers/Footers; Print Preview* (Chapter 11).

_____ *Forms*

Menu Bar: Layout (Page, Paper Size)

**CUA
Keyboard:**   〈Alt〉〈F9〉

**WordPerfect
5.1 Keyboard:**   〈Shift〉〈F8〉

Description: Allows you to choose a paper definition that
compensates for wide forms.

Procedure: 1. Select Layout at any point in your document.

2. Choose Page.

3. Click on Paper Size.

4. Click on Add.

5. Scroll through the list of paper types to
create a unique paper type. (Unique means
that the type is not listed in the paper
sizes you have already defined.)

6. Click on the paper orientation boxes to
change the printer defintion to wide forms.

7. Click on OK to save the changes and return to the Paper Size window.

8. Click on Select to choose the new definition now, or click on Close to leave the

Paper Size window and choose the definition at a later time.

Note: If you selected the definition, your document
will have new default margins from the definition code forward.

See Also: *Labels* (Chapter 8); *Paper Size*.

Headers/Footers ———————————————

Menu Bar: Layout (Page, Headers or Footers)

**CUA
Keyboard:** <Alt><F9>

**WordPerfect
5.1 Keyboard:** <Shift><F8>

Description: Allows you to print the same information at
the top or bottom of every page.

Procedure: 1. Select Layout at the beginning of the first
page on which you want the header or
footer to appear.

2. Choose Page.

3. Click on Header (for text to be printed at
the top of the page) or Footer (for text to
be printed at the bottom of the page).

4. You can have two headers and two footers in a document; Header or Footer A
simply refers to the first one, which you
will select if this is the first header or
footer you are creating. If your header/
footer already exists and you want to
change it, choose edit or discontinue.

5. Type or edit the text for the header or
footer. You can use the Font Menu to provide attributes for the text.

6. Click on Placement to determine whether the header/footer will appear on every page or odd or even pages only. Click on OK to save the placement changes.

7. Using the Layout commands, determine where you want the page number to appear on the page. Click on Page Number. ^B will appear.

8. Click on Close to save the changes and return to the document.

9. Select Layout/Page/Numbering to change the default page number and style. Since you have already defined the page numbering in the header/footer, do not redefine it in the Define Page Numbering box.

10. Click on OK to save the changes and return to your document. The header/ footer will be in effect from this point forward; it will not affect pages before the header/footer code.

Notes:

1. When you edit a header/footer, Word-Perfect works backward through the document to the first header/footer code it can find, not the first header/footer code in the document.

2. If a header does not print on the page you have positioned the code on, try moving the header code to the bottom of the previous page.

3. You can have both headers and footers on the same page.

See Also: *Page Numbering* (Chapter 5).

Landscape Paper Orientation _____

See *Portrait/Landscape*.

Move Text _____

See *Cut; Paste*.

Outline _____

Menu Bar:	Tools (Outline)
CUA Keyboard:	<Alt><Shift><F5>
WordPerfect 5.1 Keyboard:	<Shift><F5>
Description:	Allows you to automatically number up to eight levels in an outline in several different styles, including legal and user-defined.

Table 4.1.   Outline Default Options

Option	Default
Predefined Format	Outline
Style	I., A., 1., a., (1), (a), (i), a)
Starting Outline Number	1
Attach Previous Level	No
Current Outline Style	None
Enter Inserts Paragraph Number	Enabled
Auto Adjust to Current Level	Enabled
Outline On	Enabled

Procedure for Creating or Changing the Numbering Style of an Outline:

1. Select Tools at the point in your document where you want to begin outlining.

2. Choose Outline.

3. Click on Define.

4. Use the scroll bar to select the predefined format you want. Choose an option by pressing the number next to it.

5. Click on Change.

6. Highlight the desired style and click on Select.

7. Click on any option you wish to toggle on or off.

8. Click on OK to save the changes and return to the document. Outlining is turned on unless you turned the toggle off.

Procedure for Creating the Outline:

Skip steps 1 and 2 if you have just created the numbering style for your outline.

1. Select Tools.

2. Choose Outline.

3. Click on Outline On.

4. Press <Enter> to insert the first paragraph number.

5. Press <Tab> once for each outline level.

6. Press Indent, or the space bar plus the <Tab> key, to indent the text from the number.

7. Type the text.

8. Repeat steps 3 through 6 until the outline is finished.

9. Select Tools.

10. Click on Outline Off.

Procedure to Restart Numbering:

1. Select Tools at the point in your outline where you want to change the number.

2. Choose Outline

3. Click on Define.

4. Choose Starting Outline Number to change the number and/or level.

5. Click on OK to save your changes and return to your Outline screen.

Note: An outline can be easily restructured by moving the cursor to the outline number and tabbing or using the backspace key to change the level. If you accidentally delete the [Page Num] code, turn on the outline feature again at the point where the code was accidentally deleted and press <Enter>.

See Also: Paragraph Numbering.

Page, Conditional End of

See *Conditional End of Page*.

Paragraph Numbering

Menu Bar: Tools (Paragraph Number)

CUA Keyboard: <Alt><F5>

WordPerfect 5.1 Keyboard: <Shift><F5>

Description: Allows you to number your paragraphs (or outline) one number at a time.

Procedure:
1. Select Tools at the beginning of the paragraph or line you want to number.

2. Choose Outline.

3. Choose Paragraph Number.

4. Click on Insert to insert an automatic paragraph number, which will change one level every time you press <Tab>. If you want a fixed number whose level cannot be changed, click on Manual and enter a level number.

5. Repeat these steps every time you want to number a paragraph or line in your document.

Note: If you use automatic paragraph numbering, the numbers are renumbered each time you insert an additional paragraph in the document; the same is true if you delete a paragraph.

See Also: *Outline; Page Numbering* (Chapter 5).

_____ *Paper Size*

Menu Bar:	Layout (Page, Paper Size)
CUA Keyboard:	<Alt><F9>
WordPerfect 5.1 Keyboard:	<Shift><F8>
Description:	Allows you to select different kinds of paper (envelopes, labels, letterhead) and orientation (landscape or portrait).
WordPerfect Defaults:	8½″ by 11″ Portrait
Procedure:	1. Select Layout at the point in your document where you want the paper size to change.
	2. Choose Page.
	3. Click on Paper Size.

4. Drag the scroll bar through the list of defined paper sizes and orientations.

5. If your desired paper size and orientation combination is not there, double-click on Add to see if you can combine the defined options. If your paper size and orientation combination is there, highlight it and click on Select to save the changes and return to your document.

   a. If you selected Add, change the options shown to define the style you need. Move the cursor to the paper type and orientation you want. Then click on OK to save the changes and return to the Paper Size options screen.

   b. Select the newly defined paper size/orientation and click on Select to return to your document.

   c. The [ALL OTHERS] definition is meant to be used if WordPerfect cannot match the definition you want. If your definition is not there, double click on [ALL OTHERS] and enter your own definitions. When finished, click on OK to save the new definition and return to the Paper Size options screen. Then highlight the new definition and click on Select to save the changes and return to your document.

Notes: 1. Your document will now have new default margins forced by the new paper size from the beginning of this page forward.

See Also: Labels (Chapter 8).

Paste

Menu Bar:	Edit (Paste)
CUA Keyboard:	<Shift><Insert>
WordPerfect 5.1 Keyboard:	Not Available
Description:	Allows you to move text from one location to another.
Procedure:	1. Block and Cut the text that you want moved.
	2. Move the cursor to the location where you want the cut text to be inserted.
	3. Select Edit/Paste. The text will appear in the new location.
Notes:	This command will only work if the text in question was the very last deletion made with the Cut command. If not (if you used the <Delete> key without the <Shift> key, for example), use the Undelete key to restore the text.
Shortcut:	To retrieve cut text, press <Ctrl>V.
See Also:	*Cut; Undelete*.

Portrait/Landscape

Menu Bar:	Layout (Page, Paper Size)
CUA Keyboard:	<Alt><F9>
WordPerfect 5.1 Keyboard:	<Shift><F8>

Description: Allows you to select a different orientation (landscape or portrait) for your document.

**WordPerfect
Default:**   Portrait

Procedure:
1. Select Layout at the point in your document where you want a different page orientation.
2. Choose Page.
3. Click on Paper Size.
4. Highlight the appropriate paper orientation.

Note: Your document from this page forward will have new default margins forced by the new paper size.

See Also: *Labels* (Chapter 8); *Paper Size*, to create a different landscape or portrait definition.

Protect Block

See *Block Protect*.

Reveal Codes, Using

Menu Bar: View (Reveal Codes)

Feature Keys: <Alt><F3>

Description: Allows you to view the formatting features that you have put into a specified document. WordPerfect hides all codes in the normal screen so that you can focus on the document. <Alt><F3> is a toggle. You can turn reveal codes on or off at any point in your document.

See Also: *Deleting Codes; Reveal Codes* (Chapter 1);
Reveal Codes Colors (Chapter 2).

_____ *Reveal Codes Window, Changing Size*

Menu Bar: Not Available

**Function
Keys:**   Not Available

Mouse: Lower right-hand corner, Scroll Bar

Description: Allows you to change the size of the Reveal
Codes window.

Procedure: 1. Move the mouse to the corner of the black
space below the down arrow on the
scroll bar.

2. The cursor will change to a double-headed
arrow. Click and drag the black space
(which now appears as a black line) to the
desired position.

3. The Reveal Codes window now appears,
with a window as large as you indicated.
You can toggle off Reveal Codes by pressing <Alt><F3>.

4. To change the Reveal Codes window back
to its original size, position the mouse at
any point on the bar dividing the Reveal
Codes and Document windows. After the
cursor changes to a double-headed arrow,
drag the line to the old position.

_____ *Save Block*

Menu Bar: File (Save)

CUA
Keyboard: <Shift><F3>

WordPerfect
5.1 Keyboard: <F10>

Description: Allows you to save a block of text as a sepa-
                   rate file. The text remains part of the original
                   document.

Procedure: 1. Block the text you want to save separately.
                   2. Select File.
                   3. Choose Save.
                   4. Type in the name of the blocked text and
                      click on Save.

Note: If you want the newly saved block to be de-
                   leted from the original text, delete it while it
                   is still highlighted.

See Also: *Cut; Save* (Chapter 3); *Save As* (Chapter 3).

Summary

See *Document Summary*.

Typeover

Menu Bar: Not Available

Function
Keys: <Insert>

Description: Allows you to type over existing text. The
                   <Insert> key is a toggle key. Press it once to
                   turn the feature on; press it again to turn the
                   feature off.

Undelete

Menu Bar:	Edit (Undelete)
CUA Keyboard:	⟨Alt⟩⟨Shift⟩←
WordPerfect 5.1 Keyboard:	⟨F3⟩
Description:	Allows you to retrieve up to your last three deletions.
Procedure:	1. Select the Edit Menu.
	2. Choose Undelete. Your most-recently deleted text will appear highlighted on the screen. A box will prompt you to restore this deletion or to see the previous deletion.
	3. Press Restore to retrieve the deletion you want.
See Also:	*Undo*.

Undo

Menu Bar:	Edit (Undo)
CUA Keyboard:	⟨Alt⟩⟨←⟩ or ⟨Ctrl⟩⟨Z⟩
WordPerfect 5.1 Keyboard:	⟨Ctrl⟩⟨Z⟩
Description:	Allows you to reinstate your last change.
Procedure:	1. Select the Edit Menu.
	2. Choose Undo. Your very last action (typed words, a deletion) will be reversed. For example, if you deleted a word, it will ap-

pear; if you typed a word, it will disap-
pear.

See Also: *Undelete*.

Widow/Orphan _____

Menu Bar:	Layout (Page, Widow/Orphan)
CUA Keyboard:	<Alt><F9>
WordPerfect 5.1 Keyboard:	<Shift><F8>

Description: Allows you to prevent the occurrence of wid-
ows (the first line of a paragraph on the last
line of a page) and orphans (the last line of a
paragraph on the first line of a page).

**WordPerfect
Default:**   Off

Procedure: 1. Select Layout at the point in your document where you want to change the
Widow/Orphan setting.

2. Choose Page.

3. Click on Widow/Orphan. A code is inserted at the beginning of the line to prevent it from being by itself at the top or
bottom of a page.

See Also: *Block Protect; Conditional End of Page*.

5

Layout

The commands in this chapter allow you to manipulate the way a document will look when it is completed. Some commands can fit either in *Manipulating the Page* (Chapter 4) or in *Layout* (Chapter 5). Generally speaking, if the command or feature involves adding or deleting text to the file, it is in Chapter 4; if the command or feature deals strictly with appearance, it is in Chapter 5.

Arabic Page Numbers

See *Page Numbering*.

Beginning Font

See *Font, Initial*.

Bold

Menu Bar:	Font
Function Keys:	<Ctrl>b
Description:	Allows you to change the appearance of selected text.
Procedure:	1. Highlight the text you want to bold.
	2. Press <Ctrl>b.

Note:	To change the document font to bold, use the Font menu.
See Also:	*Font Attributes*.

Capitalization of Existing Text _____

See *Convert Case*.

Capitalization of New Text _____

Menu Bar:	Not Available
Function Keys:	<Caps Lock>
Description:	Allows you to type new text in all capitals.
Procedure:	1. Move the cursor to the point where you want to capitalize text.
	2. Press the <Caps Lock> key.
	3. Type the text.
	4. Press the <Caps Lock> key again.
See Also:	*Convert Case*.

Center Line _____

Menu Bar:	Layout (Line, Center)
CUA Keyboard:	<Shift><F7>
WordPerfect 5.1 Keyboard:	<Shift><F6>
Description:	Allows you to center the current line.

WordPerfect
Default: Off

Procedure: 1. Position the cursor at the beginning of the
                      line you want centered.
                   2. Select Layout.
                   3. Choose Line.
                   4. Click on Center.

Notes: 1. You can center a block of text by highlight-
                      ing it and using the Center command.
                   2. To center text over a specific point on a
                      line, tab or space to the desired position,
                      turn on Center, and begin typing.

_____ *Center Page Top to Bottom*

See *Center Page* (Chapter 11).

_____ *Center Text*

See *Center Line*.

_____ *Columns, Newspaper or Parallel*

Menu Bar: Layout (Columns, Define)

CUA
Keyboard: <Alt><Shift><F9>

WordPerfect
5.1 Keyboard: <Alt><F7>

Description: Allows you to divide your page into horizon-
                   tal (parallel) or vertical (newspaper) rows.

Table 5.1. Column Defaults

Setting	Default
Number of Columns	2
Type	Newspaper
Options	Evenly Spaced: Enabled
	Columns On: Enabled
Margins	1″ - 4″
	4.5″ - 7.5″
Distance Between Columns	0.5″

Procedure:

1. Select the Layout Menu at the point in your document where you want the text to flow in columns.

2. Choose Columns.

3. Click on Define.

4. Change any settings you want.

5. Click on OK to save the changes and return to your document. Columns are now on unless you disabled that option.

6. To turn columns off, move the cursor to the beginning of the text that you want formatted differently and select Layout/Columns/Columns Off.

Notes:

1. Once the column definition has been set for a document, it is in effect and will not have to be redefined again for that document unless you want to change one of the settings in the Define Column box (Table 5.1). You can turn columns on and off through the Layout/Columns/Column On-Off Menu.

2. You can use this command with or without already-existing text on the screen. If text is on the screen, define and turn on the columns at the desired point, then move

the cursor to the end of the desired column and click on Columns Off.

Shortcut: Use the Ruler Bar Columns icon (below the Window Menu) to select the number of newspaper-style columns you want and to turn the column on.

See Also: *Ruler Bar Columns; Display* (Chapter 2).

_____ *Convert Case*

Menu Bar: Edit (Convert Case, Uppercase or Lowercase)

Function Keys: Not Available

Description: Allows you to convert existing text from lowercase to all capitals (or vice versa).

Procedure:
1. Block the text you want converted to all capitals or all lowercase.
2. Select Edit.
3. Choose Convert Case.
4. Click on Uppercase or Lowercase.

Note: When you convert text to lowercase, only characters that follow periods will be capitalized by WordPerfect. This means that names and titles will have to be manually recapitalized after the conversion.

See Also: *Capitalization of New Text*.

_____ *Dash*

See *Special Codes*.

Decimal Alignment Character ────────────

See *Special Codes*.

Display Pitch ──────────────────────────

Menu Bar:	Layout (Document, Display Pitch)
CUA Keyboard:	\<Ctrl\>\<Shift\>\<F9\>
WordPerfect 5.1 Keyboard:	\<Shift\>\<F8\>
Description:	Allows you to change the display pitch.
WordPerfect Default:	Automatic
Procedure:	1. Select Layout on a blank screen or at the beginning of an existing document.
	2. Choose Document.
	3. Click on the Display Pitch.
	4. Make the changes.
	5. Click on OK to save the changes and return to your document.

Double Indent ──────────────────────────

See *Indent Left and Right*.

Flush Right ────────────────────────────

Menu Bar:	Layout (Line, Flush Right)
CUA Keyboard:	\<Alt\>\<F7\>

**WordPerfect
5.1 Keyboard:**   〈Alt〉〈F6〉

Description: Allows you to justify the current line from the right.

**WordPerfect
Default:**   Off

Procedure: 1. Position the cursor at the beginning of the line that you wish to make flush right.

2. Select Layout.

3. Choose Line.

4. Click on Flush Right.

Notes: 1. Tabs will be lost when you use this command.

2. You can also use this command when you block text.

_____ *Font Attributes*

Menu Bar: Font

**CUA
Keyboard:**   〈F9〉

**WordPerfect
5.1 Keyboard:**   〈Ctrl〉〈F8〉

Description: Allows you to change the typeface and the font appearance and size of selected text. You can also change the font for the whole document or from any point in the document.

Table 5.2. WordPerfect Font Attributes

Appearance	Size
Bold, Underline, Double Underline, Italic, Outline, Shadow, Small Cap, Redline, Strikeout	Superscript, Subscript, Fine, Small, Large, Very Large, Extra Large

Procedure:
1. Highlight the text whose attributes you want to change. If you want to change the type from this point forward, and not just a small block of text, position the cursor at the point where you want the new font attributes to take effect.
2. Select Font.
3. Change the font, appearance, and size of the highlighted type by clicking on the appropriate boxes.
4. Click on OK to save the changes and return to the document. The highlighted text now has the new attributes.

Note: If you frequently change fonts, you can assign the font to the ruler for quicker access. Click on Assign to Ruler, then highlight the fonts that you want on the ruler Font Menu and add them to the list. (You can also double-click on the Ruler Bar Font icon to go to the Assign to Ruler Menu.)

Shortcuts:
1. To use bold, italics, or underline: Highlight the text and press <Ctrl>b, <Ctrl>i, or <Ctrl>u.
2. To use Double Underline, Redline, Strikeout, or Subscript or Superscript: Highlight the text, go to the Font Menu, and click on the desired option.

3. To change text to a percentage of the default font size: Highlight the text, press
<Ctrl>S, and select the desired size.

See Also: *Bold; Font, Initial; Italics; Ruler Bar Font
and Size; Type Size, Changing; Underline.*

Font, Changing

See *Font Attributes*.

Font, Initial

Menu Bar: Layout (Document, Initial Font)

**CUA
Keyboard:**   <Ctrl><Shift><F9>

**WordPerfect
5.1 Keyboard:**   <Shift><F8>

Description: Allows you to change the beginning font for
the document.

**WordPerfect
Default:**   12-Point Courier

Procedure: 1. Select Layout on a blank screen or at the
beginning of an existing document.

2. Choose Document.

3. Click on Initial Font.

4. Scroll through the list of available fonts
(defined by your printer selection) and
click on the desired typeface and type size.

5. Click on OK to save the changes and return to your document.

Shortcut: Go to the beginning of the document and
choose a font and size from the Ruler Bar. If

no other fonts are in the document, this effectively changes the font for the entire file.

See Also: *Ruler Bar Font and Size.*

Font, Kerning

See *Kerning.*

Force Odd/Even Page

See *Page Numbering.*

Hanging Paragraph

Menu Bar:	Layout (Paragraph, Hanging Indent)
CUA Keyboard:	<Ctrl><F7>
WordPerfect 5.1 Keyboard:	<F4><Shift><Tab>
Description:	Allows you to have a paragraph in which only the first line is not indented.
Procedure:	1. Select Layout at the point where you want the hanging paragraph.
	2. Choose Paragraph.
	3. Click on Hanging Indent.
	4. Type your text. The first line will begin at the left margin; the rest will be indented.
Note:	Existing paragraphs can be indented by moving your cursor to the beginning of the paragraph and pressing hanging indent, as long as you did not use <Enter> to manually wrap the lines.

See Also: *Indent; Indent Left and Right.*

Hard Space

See *Special Codes*.

Hard Tab

See *Special Codes*.

Height

See *Line Height*.

Hyphenation

Menu Bar:	Layout (Line, Hyphenation)
CUA Keyboard:	\<Shift\>\<F9\>
WordPerfect 5.1 Keyboard:	\<Shift\>\<F8\>
Description:	Allows you to turn on hyphenation and change the hyphenation zone.
WordPerfect Defaults:	*Hyphenation:* Off
	Hyphenation Zone: Left: 10%, Right: 4%
Procedure:	1. Select Layout at the beginning of the paragraph where you want hyphenation to begin.
	2. Choose Line.
	3. Click on Hyphenation.

4. Click on the Turn On Hyphenation box to enable hyphenation. Insert new numbers in the Hyphenation Zone box to change the hyphenation zone.

5. Click on OK to save the changes and return to your document.

6. To turn off hyphenation, return to Layout/Line/Hyphenation and Click on the Turn On Hyphenation box, removing the X.

Hyphenation Codes, Inserting _____

See *Special Codes*.

Hyphenation Zone, Changing _____

See *Hyphenation*.

Indent _____

Menu Bar:	Layout (Paragraph, Indent)
CUA Keyboard:	\<F7\>
WordPerfect 5.1 Keyboard:	\<F4\>
Description:	Allows you to indent an entire paragraph from the left margin.
Procedure:	1. Select Layout at the beginning of the paragraph you want indented.
	2. Choose Page.
	3. Click on Indent. The paragraph will be indented one tab stop. Repeat if you want the paragraph indented further.

4. Type your paragraph. The indent will remain in effect until you press ⟨Enter⟩.

Note: Existing paragraphs can be indented by moving your cursor to the beginning of the paragraph and pressing indent, as long as you did
not use ⟨Enter⟩ to manually wrap the lines.

See Also: *Hanging Paragraph; Indent Left and Right;
Tabs, Set.*

_____ *Indent Left and Right*

Menu Bar: Layout (Paragraph, Double Indent)

**CUA
Keyboard:**   ⟨Ctrl⟩⟨Shift⟩⟨F7⟩

**WordPerfect
5.1 Keyboard:**   ⟨Shift⟩⟨F4⟩

Description: Allows a paragraph to be indented equally
from the left and right margins.

Procedure: 1. Select Layout at the beginning of the paragraph you want indented.

2. Choose Paragraph.

3. Click on Double Indent. The paragraph
will be indented one tab stop from each
side for each time you select Double Indent.

4. Type your paragraph. The left and right
indent will remain in effect until you press
⟨Enter⟩.

Note: Existing paragraphs can be indented from the
left and right by moving the cursor to the beginning of the paragraph and selecting Double Indent, as long as you did not use ⟨Enter⟩
to manually wrap the lines.

See Also: *Hanging Paragraph; Indent; Tabs, Set*

Insert Page Number in Text _____

See *Page Numbering*.

Italics _____

Menu Bar:	Font (Italic)
Function Keys:	\<Ctrl\>i
Description:	Allows you to change the appearance of selected text.
Procedure:	1. Highlight the text you want to italicize.
	2. Press \<Ctrl\>i.
Note:	To change the document font to italics, use the Font menu.
See Also:	*Font Attributes*.

Justification _____

Menu Bar:	Layout (Justification)
Function Keys:	Not Available
Description:	Allows you to decide whether you want the text to be even on the left, the right, both left and right (full), or centered.
WordPerfect Default:	Left
Procedure:	1. Select Layout at the beginning of the paragraph where you want the different justification to begin, or highlight the text you want to change.
	2. Choose Justification.

3. Click on the setting that you want. The new justification is in effect from this point forward. If you highlighted text, only the selected type has been changed.

Shortcuts: Click on the Justification icon (under the Help Menu) on the Ruler Bar at the point where you want to change the justification type. Also, you can use <Ctrl>l, <Ctrl>r, <Ctrl>j (Center), and <Ctrl>f at any point in your document.

Note: The justification code is placed at the beginning of a page unless you select text for justification. (If you want justification to take place at the location you indicate, change the Auto Code Placement default.)

See Also: *Environment* (Chapter 2) for Auto Code Placement; *Ruler Bar Justification*.

_____ *Kerning*

Menu Bar: Layout (Typesetting)

**Function
Keys:** Not Available

Description: Allows you to change the spacing of certain letter combinations.

**WordPerfect
Default:** Off

Procedure: 1. Select Layout at the point in your document where you want to turn on kerning.

2. Click on Typesetting.

3. The Typesetting Dialog Box will appear. Click on Automatic Kerning to have WordPerfect change the letter combination

spacing, or choose Manual Kerning and enter the spacing yourself.

4. Click on OK to save the changes and return to the Typesetting Dialog Box.

5. Click on OK to return to your document.

Note: You cannot use kerning if you are printing with Windows printer drivers.

See Also: *Printer Commands* (Chapter 11).

Labels

See *Labels* (Chapter 8).

Left and Right Margins

See *Margins*.

Line Height

Menu Bar:	Layout (Line, Height)
CUA Keyboard:	<Shift><F9>
WordPerfect 5.1 Keyboard:	<Shift><F8>
Description:	Allows you to specify a different line height for the current document.
Procedure:	1. Select Layout at the beginning of the paragraph where you want to change the height of the line.

2. Choose Line.

3. Click on Height.

4. Click on Fixed and enter a new number. The default is the standard height of the type; that is, 10-point type is .167″ high.

5. Click on OK to save the changes and return to the document.

6. At the point you want the type to return to the standard height, select Layout/Line/ Height and click on Auto; then click on OK to save the changes.

Line Numbering

Menu Bar: Layout (Line, Numbering)

CUA Keyboard: <Shift><F9>

WordPerfect 5.1 Keyboard: <Shift><F8>

Description: Allows you to number each line on a page or a document.

WordPerfect Default: Off

Procedure:
1. Select Layout at the beginning of the paragraph where you want the lines numbered.

2. Choose Line.

3. Click on Numbering.

4. Drag the scroll bar to click on either Restart (each page) or Continuous.

5. Click on OK to save the changes and return to the document.

6. To discontinue Line Numbering, return to the Layout/Line/Numbering Menu and click on Off, then click on OK to save the changes.

Note:	The numbering does not show up on the Draft Mode or Default Mode screens. You can only see it through the Print Preview screen or when the document is printed.
See Also:	*Headers/Footers* (Chapter 4); *Paragraph Numbering* (Chapter 4); *Print Preview* (Chapter 11).

Line Spacing

Menu Bar:	Layout (Line, Spacing)
CUA Keyboard:	<Shift><F9>
WordPerfect 5.1 Keyboard:	<Shift><F8>
Description:	Allows you to change the amount of white space between lines in a document.
WordPerfect Default:	1
Procedure:	1. Select Layout at the beginning of the paragraph where you want to change the amount of white space.
	2. Choose Line.
	3. Click on Spacing.
	4. Enter a new number, or drag on the scroll bar to determine the amount of white space.
	5. Click on OK to save the changes and return to your document. The change will be in effect from this point forward.
	6. To return to the default, select Layout/ Line/Spacing again, and choose the num-

ber 1. Then click on OK to return to your document.

Shortcut: Use the Ruler Bar Spacing icon (far right) to change the amount of white space (between one and two lines).

See Also: *Ruler Bar Spacing.*

Lowercase Existing Text

See *Convert Case.*

Margin Release

Menu Bar: Layout (Paragraph, Margin Release)

Function Keys: <Shift><Tab>

Description: Allows you to move text into the margin.

Procedure:
1. Select Layout at the beginning of the text you want moved into the left margin.
2. Choose Paragraph.
3. Click on Margin Release. The text will be backed up into the left margin one time for each Margin Release.
4. To reverse the action, use Reveal Codes to see the [Mar Rel] Code; then delete it.

See Also: *Reveal Codes* (Chapter 4).

Margins

Menu Bar: Layout (Margins)

CUA
Keyboard: <Ctrl><F8>

WordPerfect
5.1 Keyboard: <Shift><F8>

Description: Allows you to set margins at the beginning of the document or at any point in the document.

WordPerfect
Default: 1″ all around

Procedure: 1. Select Layout at the beginning of a document or at the beginning of a paragraph or page where you want to change the margins.

2. Click on Margins.

3. Use the mouse to position the cursor to set the first margin to your needs; use <Tab> to navigate through the rest of the margin boxes.

4. Click on OK to save the changes and return to your document.

5. To return the margins to their original settings, move the cursor to the point where you want the original settings to begin again, select Layout/Margins, and enter the original numbers.

6. Click on OK to save the changes.

Note: The top/bottom margin codes will place themselves at the beginning of the page; the left and right codes place themselves at the beginning of the paragraph.

New Page Number

See *Page Numbering*.

_____ *Numbering, Line*

See *Line Numbering*.

_____ *Numbering, Page*

See *Page Numbering*.

_____ *Overstrike*

Menu Bar:	Font (Overstrike)
Function Keys:	Not Available
Description:	Allows you to create your own characters and assign to them font attributes.
Procedure:	1. Select Font at the point in your document where you want the special characters.
	2. Choose Overstrike.
	3. Click on Create to create your own characters, or Edit to modify characters you have already created.
	4. Enter the characters you want to combine.
	5. Add attributes by dragging on the arrow scroll bar. Be sure that your new characters are between the on/off font attribute codes.
	6. Click on OK to save the changes and return to the document. The new character appears at the cursor.
Note:	The printed appearance of your overstruck character depends on the capabilities of your printer.

Page Break _____

Menu Bar:	Layout (Page, Page Break)
Function Keys:	\<Ctrl\>\<Enter\>
Description:	Allows you to determine where your pages end and begin. WordPerfect automatically inserts a page break at the end of X number of lines, where X depends on the paper and font sizes. You can force a new page to begin anywhere you want.
Procedure:	1. Select Layout at the point in your document where you want a new page to begin.
	2. Choose Page.
	3. Click on Page Break. A new page begins at that point, as indicated by the numbers in the lower right-hand corner.
	4. To reverse the action, use Reveal Codes to locate the [HPg] Code, and then delete it.
See Also:	*Block Protect* (Chapter 4) to keep text within a set of codes together; *Conditional End of Page* (Chapter 4); *Widow/Orphan* (Chapter 4).

Page, Force Odd/Even _____

See *Page Numbering*.

Page Format, Suppress _____

See *Suppress Page Format*.

Page Numbering

Menu Bar:	Layout (Page, Numbering)

**CUA
Keyboard:**   <Alt><F9>

**WordPerfect
5.1 Keyboard:**   <Shift><F8>

Description: Allows you to automatically number your pages, change your numbering type (Arabic or Roman), insert an automatic page number into the text, or force the current page to be odd or even.

Table 5.3. Page Numbering Defaults

Default	Settings
Page Number Position	Off
Insert Page Number	Off
Numbering Type	1, 2, 3, 4
New Page Number	Current
Force Current Page Odd/Even	Off

Procedure:
1. Select Layout at the top of the page whose number you want to change.
2. Choose Page.
3. Click on Numbering.
4. Change the options as necessary:
   a. Use the Position scroll bar to determine where page numbers will print. (Do not use this option if you have already defined page numbers in the header/footer. Being different codes, both page numbering definitions will print.)
   b. To change the numbering type from Arabic to Roman, drag the Numbering Type scroll bar to the desired number-

ing type. If you want a new page number beginning with this page, enter it at the New Page Number box. (This will reset any earlier numbering type definitions.)

c. To insert a page number at the current cursor position on the page, click on Insert Page Number.

d. If you want the current page to have an even or odd number, click on the Odd or Even box.

5. When all changes have been made, click on OK to save the changes and return to the document. Your changes will be in effect from this point forward.

6. To reverse the action, return to the Layout/Page/Numbering Menu and change the choices. Alternatively, use Reveal Codes to find and delete the page number codes.

Notes:

1. ^B always refers to the current page. Use Cross Reference to insert a page number other than the current one into the text.

2. If the page numbering or new number does not appear on the first page that you have indicated, move the Page Numbering or New Page Number code to the bottom of the previous page.

See Also: *Cross-Reference* (Chapter 7); *Headers/Footers* (Chapter 4).

Redline Method _____

Menu Bar: Layout (Document, Redline Method)

CUA
Keyboard: <Ctrl><Shift><F9>

WordPerfect
5.1 Keyboard: <Shift><F8>

Description: Allows you to determine how redline will
                    look when it is printed.

WordPerfect
Default: Printer Dependent

Procedure: 1. Select Layout at any point in your docu-
                       ment.

                   2. Choose Document.

                   3. Click on Redline Methods.

                   4. Click on the method that you want.

                   5. Click on OK to save the changes and re-
                      turn to your document.

See Also: *Redline/Strikeout*.

Redline/Strikeout

Menu Bar: Font (Redline, Strikeout)

Function
Keys: Not Available

Description: Allows you to indicate new (with redline) or
                    deleted (with strikeout) text in a document.

WordPerfect
Default: Printer Dependent

Procedure: 1. Position the cursor at the beginning of the
                      text you want to Redline or Strikeout.

                   2. Block the text, positioning the cursor at the
                      end of the text you want to Redline or
                      Strikeout.

                   3. Select Font.

4. Click on Redline or Strikeout. The text is given the additional attributes.

Notes: 1. Alternatively, you can select Redline before the text is added, then use the arrow key to move beyond the Font Attribute Off code when you are through adding text.

2. Redline/Strikeout is also used by the Document Compare feature, which compares a document on the screen with a previously-saved document on disk.

3. How Redline appears on your printed documents depends upon the capabilities of your printer (run PRINTER.TST in the wpwin directory) and on how you defined the Redline Method in the Layout Menu. A line can appear in the left margin or in alternating left and right margins.

See Also: *Document Compare* (Chapter 3); *Document Defaults* (Chapter 2).

Roman Page Numbers

See *Page Numbering*.

Ruler Bar

Menu Bar: View (Ruler)

CUA Keyboard: <Alt><Shift><F3>

WordPerfect 5.1 Keyboard: <Shift><F11>

Description: Allows you to toggle the ruler on and off.

WordPerfect
Default: On

Procedure: 1. Select View at any point in your docu-
                       ment.

                    2. Click on Ruler to toggle the ruler on
                       and off.

See Also: *Ruler Bar* (Chapter 1).

                    Environment (Chapter 2) to change the Ruler
                    Bar defaults.

                    Ruler Bar Columns; Ruler Bar Font and Size;
                    Ruler Bar Justification; Ruler Bar Spacing;
                    Ruler Bar Styles; Ruler Bar Tab; Ruler Bar
                    Tables.

_____ *Ruler Bar Columns*

Menu Bar: Not Available

Function
Keys: Not Available

Description: Allows you to quickly specify and turn on be-
                    tween two and five newspaper-type columns
                    in your text.

Procedure: 1. Move the cursor to the point where you
                       want the newspaper columns to begin.

                    2. Use the mouse to click and drag on the
                       column box on the Ruler Bar (below the
                       Window Menu). You have the option of
                       choosing two, three, four, or five newspa-
                       per-type columns. Once you have clicked
                       on an column option, columns are
                       turned on.

                    3. To turn off columns, use Reveal Codes to
                       locate the [Col Off] code and move the
                       cursor beyond it. Alternatively, go to the

Layout/Tables Menu to turn off columns at the point in your document where columns are no longer desired.

See Also: *Columns, Newspaper or Parallel; Tables* (Chapter 9).

Ruler Bar Font and Size

Menu Bar: Not Available

Function Keys: Not Available

Description: Allows you to quickly change the font and type size of selected text, or to change the font for the document.

Procedure: 1. Assign your most-used fonts to the ruler with the following steps:

a. Select Font at any point in your document.

b. Choose Font.

c. Click on Assign to Ruler.

d. Highlight each font you want to assign to the ruler and click on Add.

e. Click on OK to save the changes and return to the Font Menu.

f. Click on OK to leave the Font Menu.

2. Move the cursor to the point you want the new font to take effect, or highlight the text to be changed.

3. Click on the Ruler Bar Font, dragging to select the desired font. The new font is in effect.

4. If you want a different type size, click and drag on the Ruler Bar Size to select

the new type size. The new size is in effect.

Shortcut: Double-click on the Ruler Bar Font icon to go
to the Font Dialog Box and assign fonts to the
Ruler Bar.

See Also: *Font Attributes*.

_____ *Ruler Bar Justification*

Menu Bar: Not Available

**Function
Keys:** Not Available

Description: Allows you to change the justification of a selected block of text or for the document from
this point forward.

Procedure: 1. Highlight the text you want justified, or
position the cursor at the point where you
want to change the justification of the document.

2. Use the mouse to click and drag on the
Justification icon (below the Help Menu)
on the Ruler Bar. Select an option. The
new justification is now in effect.

3. To change to another setting, repeat steps
1 and 2.

See Also: *Justification*.

_____ *Ruler Bar Size*

See *Ruler Bar Font and Size*.

Ruler Bar Spacing _____

Menu Bar:	Not Available
Function Keys:	Not Available
Description:	Allows you to quickly change the line spacing of a block of text or for the document from this point forward.
Procedure:	1. Highlight the text you want spaced differently, or position the cursor at the point where you want to change the spacing of the document.
	2. Use the mouse to click and drag on the Spacing icon (extreme right) of the Ruler Bar. Select an option. The new spacing number appears and is in effect from this point forward.
Note:	If you want more than double spacing, use the Layout/Line/Spacing Menu to change the spacing for the highlighted text or document.
See Also:	*Line Spacing*.

Ruler Bar Styles _____

Menu Bar:	Not Available
Function Keys:	Not Available
Description:	Allows you to quickly select a style for the current document.
Procedure:	At the point in the document where you want the new style to begin, click and drag on Ruler Bar Styles. All of the currently defined styles are located there.

Note: To define a style, use the Layout/Styles
                   Menu.

See Also: *Styles*.

_____ *Ruler Bar Tab*

Menu Bar: Not Available

**Function
Keys:**   Not Available

Description: Allows you to set new tabs. Four tab icons
                   exist (left, center, right, and decimal), along
                   with a dot leader box.

Procedure: 1. Move the cursor to the point where you
                   want the new tab. Determine what kind of
                   tab you want. If you want a tab with dot
                   leaders, for example, click on the icon at
                   the extreme left of the Ruler Bar, under the
                   Edit Menu. (The dot leader icon is a tog-
                   gle. Click on it to turn it on; click on it to
                   turn it off.)

                   2. Click and drag one of the tab icons on the
                   Ruler Bar to the new location on the ruler.
                   The tab is now set and takes effect from
                   this point forward.

Notes: 1. If you want to eliminate a tab, move the
                   cursor to the point in your document
                   where you no longer want the tab; click on
                   the tab icon on the ruler, and drag it to a
                   different location.

                   2. If you need to set a large number of tabs,
                   use the Layout/Line/Tab Set feature in-
                   stead.

See Also: *Tabs, Set*.

Ruler Bar Tables _____

Menu Bar:	Not Available
Function Keys:	Not Available
Description:	Allows you to very quickly set up a table in your document.
Procedure:	1. Move the cursor to the point in your document where you want the table to be located.
	2. Use the mouse to click and drag the grid on the Ruler Bar, located under the Macro Menu. Your table can be between 1 column by 1 row and 32 columns by 37 rows.
	3. Use the Layout/Tables Menu to modify the new table.
See Also:	*Tables* (Chapter 9).

Spaces, Underline _____

See **Underline Spaces or Tabs**.

Spacing _____

See **Line Spacing** and **Line Height**.

Special Codes _____

Menu Bar:	Layout (Line, Special Codes)
CUA Keyboard:	<Shift><F9>

WordPerfect
5.1 Keyboard: <Shift><F8>

Description: Allows you to insert certain formatting codes into the document at the cursor.

Table 5.4. WordPerfect Special Codes

Formatting Codes	Default
Hard Tab (Left, Center, Right, Decimal)	Off
Hard Tab with Dot Leaders (Left, Center, Right, Decimal)	Off
Hyphenation: Hyphen, Dash, Soft Hyphen, Hyphen Soft Return, Hyphen Ignore Word	Off
Other: Hard Space, End Centering/Alignment, Decimal Alignment Character	Off

Procedure:
1. Select Layout at the exact point in your document where you want the special formatting codes inserted.

2. Choose Line.

3. Click on Special Codes.

4. Click on the boxes of the special codes you need to insert.

5. Click on OK to insert the code into the document. You will need to repeat these steps every time you insert one of these codes into your document.

Shortcut: If you are using the same formatting code frequently, you can insert it once and then use the cut and paste operation to insert it elsewhere.

See Also: *Cut* (Chapter 4); *Paste* (Chapter 4); *Printer Commands* (Chapter 11).

Strikeout _____

See *Redline/Strikeout*.

Styles _____

Menu Bar: Layout (Styles)

**Function
Keys:**   <Alt><F8>

Description: Allows you to establish a format that can be
                  transferred to other documents. Style sheets
                  can be limited (paired) so that you are not
                  forced into a particular style for a whole doc-
                  ument, or a style sheet can define most of the
                  formatting codes you will use for one docu-
                  ment (open).

**WordPerfect
Default:**   Paired

Procedure for Creating a Style Sheet:

1. Select Layout at any point in your document.

2. Click on Styles.

3. Choose Create.

4. Click on Name and enter a short title (less
   than 20 characters) for the style sheet. Use
   <Tab> to drop to the description line, and
   enter the key words to describe the style.

5. If you need to, select Type to change the
   Style Sheet from paired to open.

6. Select Enter Key Insert (if you are creating
   a paired-type style sheet) to change the
   function of the <Enter> key while in the
   style sheet. You can change it so that
   pressing <Enter> turns off the style sheet

when you are done, or you can change it
so that ⟨Enter⟩ turns off the style sheet
and then turns it back on. You can also
leave ⟨Enter⟩ as a hard return.

7. Click on OK to save those changes and go
   to the formatting window to choose the
   formatting options for your document. If
   you are creating a paired-type style sheet,
   your screen shows a Comment: Beginning
   codes go before the Comment, and ending
   codes go after the Comment. If you are
   creating an open-type style sheet, your
   screen does not have a Comment. If, along
   the way, you decide that you want to
   change anything (such as the Enter Key Insert), click on Properties to temporarily return to that screen.

8. Click on Close to save your changes and
   return to the main Styles screen.

9. If you want to use the new style at this
   point, click on On. You will be returned to
   your document. (In order to use the paired
   style with existing text, the text whose
   style you want to change must be highlighted.)

Procedure for Editing a Style Sheet:

1. Select Layout.
2. Choose Styles.
3. Select Edit to make changes to the style
   sheet.
4. When finished, click on OK to save the
   changes and return to the document.

Procedure for Using a Style Sheet with Uncreated Text:

1. At the point that you want the new style,
   click and drag the Styles icon on the Ruler

Bar. (All defined style can be selected from there.)

2. Highlight the style sheet you want to use, and click on On. You are returned to your document with the cursor between the on/ off formatting codes.

3. Enter the text, being careful not to position the cursor on the other side of the off codes.

Procedure for Using a Style Sheet With Existing Text:

1. Block the text that you want formatted in a different style.

2. Click and drag the styles icon on the Ruler Bar.

3. Click on the style sheet you want to use.

Notes:

1. In a paired-type style sheet, you can use all formatting codes supported by Word-Perfect except those modified during a generation (Indexing, for example).

2. You can use nearly all of WordPerfect's formatting codes in an open-type style sheet, too, but you will not be able to turn them off; that is, if you put the bold for-matting code into the style sheet, the whole document will be bolded.

See Also: *Ruler Bar Styles*.

Superscript, Subscript _____

Menu Bar: Font (Superscript, Subscript)

**Function
Keys:** Not Available

Description: Allows you to turn on or off the Superscript/ Subscript option.

Procedure: 1. Highlight the text you want to be superscript or subscript.

2. Select Font.

3. Click on Superscript or Subscript.

Note: This function can also be achieved through
the Font Attributes menu.

See Also: *Font Attributes.*

Suppress Page Format

Menu Bar: Layout (Page, Suppress)

**CUA
Keyboard:** <Alt><F9>

**WordPerfect
5.1 Keyboard:** <Shift><F8>

Description: Allows you to turn off headers, footers, and
page numbering for the current page.

**WordPerfect
Default:** Off

Procedure: 1. Select Layout at the top of the page whose
formatting you want to suppress.

2. Choose Page.

3. Click on Suppress.

4. Click on the headers and footers that you
want to suppress for this page only.

5. If you want a page number printed on the
bottom center of this page, click on the
box at the bottom.

6. Click on OK to save the changes and return to your document.

Tab Codes, Inserting ―――――――――――――

See *Special Codes*.

Tabs, Align ―――――――――――――――――

See *Tabs, Set*.

Tabs, Set ――――――――――――――――――

Menu Bar: Layout (Line, Tab Set)

**CUA
Keyboard:**   <Shift><F9>

**WordPerfect
5.1 Keyboard:**   <Shift><F8>

Description: Allows you to set margins for the document.

**WordPerfect
Defaults:**   Left align, from left margin, every ½″, starting with −1″

Procedure: 1. Select Layout at the beginning of the paragraph where you want the tabs to be
changed.

2. Choose Line.

3. Choose Tab Set.

4. Decide how you want the tabs aligned,
and click on the appropriate box.

5. Decide if you want to measure from the
left margin or the left edge of the paper,
and click on the box.

6. Change the tabs by highlighting them and
clearing them, or by entering new tab settings and clicking on Tab Set.

7. Click on OK to save the changes and return to your document. The new settings are in effect from this point forward.

Shortcut: Using the Ruler Bar Tabs, click and drag the appropriate tab indicator to the point on the ruler where you want a tab. If you do not want a tab at a particular location, drag the tab icon from its existing location to a spot where you already have one.

Note: Use the Tab Set Menu to change a number of tabs; use the Ruler Bar Tabs to change one or two settings.

See Also: *Ruler Bar Tabs*.

_____ *Tabs, Underline*

See *Underline Spaces or Tabs*.

_____ *Top and Bottom Margins*

See *Margins*.

_____ *Type, Italic*

See *Italics*.

_____ *Type Size, Changing*

Menu Bar: Font (Size)

CUA Keyboard: <Ctrl>s

**WordPerfect
5.1 Keyboard:** <Ctrl><F8>

Description: Allows you to change type to a percentage of the currently used font.

Table 5.5. Size Attribute Ratios

Fine	60%
Small	80%
Large	120%
Very Large	150%
Extra Large	200%
Super/Subscript	60%

Procedure:
1. Highlight the text whose size you want to change.
2. Select Font.
3. Choose Size.
4. Click on the size you want the type to be.

Notes:
1. You can also achieve this function through the Font Attribute Menu.
2. If you have not yet entered the text, you can turn on the size attributes first, enter the text, then use Reveal Codes to move the cursor to the other side of the size code.

Shortcut: Use the Ruler Bar size icon.

See Also: *Font Attributes; Printer, Initial Settings* (Chapter 2).

Type, Special Characters _____

See *WordPerfect Characters*.

Type, Superscript or Subscript

See *Superscript, Subscript*.

Type, Underline

See *Underline*.

Underline

Menu Bar:	Font (Underline)
Function Keys:	<Ctrl>u
Description:	Allows you to change the appearance of selected text.
Procedure:	1. Highlight the text you want to underline. 2. Press <Ctrl>u.
Note:	To underline the whole document, use the Font menu. For double underlining, highlight the text and use the Font/Double Underline Menu.
See Also:	*Font Attributes*.

Underline, Double

See *Underline; Font Attributes*.

Underline Spaces or Tabs

Menu Bar:	Layout (Typesetting)

**Function
Keys:**   Not Available

Description: Allows you to underline spaces or tabs, or to
                  turn the toggle off.

**WordPerfect
Defaults:**   *Underline Spaces:* On
                  Underline Tabs: Off

Procedure: 1. Select Layout at the point in your docu-
                     ment where you want to change the tab or
                     space underlining.
                  2. Click on Typesetting.
                  3. The Typesetting Dialog Box will appear.
                     Click on Underline Spaces or Underline
                     Tab boxes to toggle them on or off.
                  5. Click on OK to save the changes and re-
                     turn to your document.

Notes: You cannot use this typesetting command if
                  you are printing with Windows printer
                  drivers.

WordPerfect Characters _____

Menu Bar: Font (WP Characters)

**CUA
Keyboard:**   <Ctrl>W

**WordPerfect
5.1 Keyboard:**   Not Available

Description: Allows you to insert nonkeyboard characters
                  (such as bullets) into your document.

**WordPerfect
Default:**   ASCII

Procedure: 1. At the point in your document where you
want to insert the special character, select
Fonts.

2. Choose WP Characters.

3. Use the Set scroll bar to highlight the
typeface you want.

4. Move the cursor to the character in the
Character Box that you want to use.

5. If the cursor is at the point in your document where you want the new character
inserted, click on Insert (if this is only one
of several characters that you want to insert into the document), or Insert and
Close (if this is the only one or the last
character you want to insert). If the cursor
is not at the point in your document where
you want it, move the cursor to the desired location before pressing Insert or Insert and Close.

Note: While the characters will always show up in
your document on the screen, they will show
up on the printed document only if your
printer supports them.

6

Search, Replace, Speller, Thesaurus, and Word Count

This chapter deals with the WordPerfect features that enable you to find specified files, find and replace text, check your spelling, and count the number of words in a specified document.

Find a File

See *Find a File* (Chapter 3).

Find Words

See *Find a File* (Chapter 3).

Look Up

See *Thesaurus*.

Replace

Menu Bar:	Edit (Replace)
CUA Keyboard:	⟨Ctrl⟩⟨F2⟩
WordPerfect 5.1 Keyboard:	⟨Alt⟩⟨F2⟩

Description: Allows you to locate and replace one text string with another throughout a document.

Procedure:
1. Select Edit from anywhere in your document.

2. Click on Replace.

3. Enter the text string you want to replace in the Search For box. If you are searching for WordPerfect codes:

   a. Click on the Codes box.

   b. Scroll through the list of codes, high-lighting the one or the ones you need.

   c. Click on Insert to make the code part of the text string.

4. Use the ⟨Tab⟩ key to get to the Replace With box. Enter the text string you want to use. You can use the codes here, also.

5. If you want the search and replace limited to the document body, click on Search Document Body Only.

6. If you want to search backward from the current cursor location, click and drag on the direction box until Backward appears. (This setting will be in effect for future searches until you change it or exit WordPerfect.)

7. When all options have been resolved satisfactorily, you have two options:

   a. Click on Replace All to replace all instances of the text string (from this point forward or backward). Word-Perfect will not ask you to confirm each replacement, which will be done automatically.

   b. Click on Search Next to find the next instance of the text string. WordPerfect will find the next instance of the text string and wait for you to either click on Replace or click on Search Next again.

Notes: 1. If your text string appears in different forms throughout your document, always use the Search Next/Replace option. If your replacement text is lowercase and the text string you are searching for sometimes has initial capitals, the document will end up with the new text string in lowercase.

2. If you want the text string deleted instead of replaced, press Search Next or Replace All when prompted for a text string to replace the existing text string.

See Also: *Search*.

_____ *Search*

Menu Bar: Edit (Search)

**Function
Keys:**   <F2>

Description: Allows you to search forward or backward for a specified text string.

**WordPerfect
Default:**   Search Forward

Procedure: 1. Select Edit from anywhere in your document.

2. Click on Search.

3. In the box, enter the desired text string. If you are searching for WordPerfect codes:

   a. Click on the Codes box.

          b. Scroll through the list of codes, high-lighting the one or ones you need.

          c. Click on Insert to make the code part of the text string.

4. If you want to limit the search to the document body (without including headers, footers, or indexing, for example) click on Search on Document Body Only.

5. If you want to search backward from the current cursor location, click and drag on the direction box until Backward appears. (This setting will be in effect for future searches until you change it or exit WordPerfect.)

6. When all options have been resolved satisfactorily, click on OK to begin the search. WordPerfect will find the next instance of the text string.

See Also: *Replace*.

Search Next

Menu Bar:	Edit (Search Next)
Function Keys:	\<Shift\>\<F2\>
Description:	Allows you to search for the next instance of a previously defined string.
WordPerfect Defaults:	All previously defined options, including the search string.
Procedure:	1. Select Edit.
	2. Click on Search Next. The search string you previously defined and used will be

the default until you change it or exit
WordPerfect.

See Also: *Search; Search Previous; Replace.*

Search Previous

Menu Bar: Edit (Search Previous)

**CUA
Keyboard:**   <Alt><F2>

**WordPerfect
5.1 Keyboard:**   <Alt><Shift><F2>

Description: Allows you to search for the prior instance of
a previously defined string.

**WordPerfect
Defaults:**   All previously defined options, including the
search string.

Procedure: 1. Select Edit.
2. Click on Search Previous. The search
string you previously defined and used
will be the default until you change it or
exit WordPerfect.

See Also: *Search; Search Next; Replace.*

Speller

Menu Bar: Tools (Speller)

**CUA
Keyboard:**   <Ctrl><F1>

**WordPerfect
5.1 Keyboard:**   <Ctrl><F2>

Description: Allows you to check the spelling of a word, page, or document.

WordPerfect Default: Spell Check Document, Suggest On

Procedure:
1. Select Tools at any point in your document (to spell check the entire document) or at any point in the word or page that you want checked. You can also highlight text to be spell checked.
2. Click on Speller.
3. The Speller Menu appears. Drag on the Check scroll bar to have WordPerfect spell check a word, a page, or selected text instead of the default.
4. Click on Start.
5. WordPerfect will check the requested text for spelling errors. Any words or character strings that do not match entries in WordPerfect's main or supplemental dictionaries will be highlighted and shown at the bottom of the Speller Menu box. If you have the Suggest option on, WordPerfect provides a list of alternate words. One of the alternate words is highlighted and appears in the Suggest box. At this point, you have several options:

   a. Click on Replace to accept the word that WordPerfect thinks is most likely.

   b. Click on one of the other words in the list to make it the replacement word, then click on Replace.

   c. Add the word to the supplemental dictionary.

   d. Click on and Skip once to have WordPerfect ignore the word. Word-

Perfect will flag the word again the next time it appears.

e. Click on Skip Always to keep Word-Perfect from flagging the word in this document. WordPerfect will still flag the word if it occurs in another document.

f. Retype the word yourself and click on Replace.

6. An announcement box will appear when the Speller is through checking the requested text. Click on OK to return to the Speller Menu.

7. To check other text in the same document, change the Check options. To leave the Speller at this point, click on Close.

Note: WordPerfect no longer gives a total word count when it is through spell checking a document.

See Also: *Word Count.*

_____ *Suggest*

See *Speller.*

_____ *Thesaurus*

Menu Bar: Tools (Thesaurus)

Function Keys: <Alt><F1>

Description: Allows you to find synonyms (words with similar meanings) or antonyms (words with opposite meanings) for currently existing text.

Procedure: 1. With the cursor on the word you want to change, select Tools.

2. Click on Thesaurus.

3. The word you are looking up appears in the Word box of the Thesaurus Menu, together with a list of synonyms and antonyms for its various forms (for example, *change* is treated as both a verb and a noun).

3. Click on the word that you want to substitute, then click on Replace; if none of the words are acceptable, you can enter another word pattern (for example, *different* for *change*) and click on Look Up. Antonyms and synonyms for the second word will appear.

4. When you finish with Thesaurus, click on Close to return to your document.

See Also: *View* (Chapter 3).

View

See *View* (Chapter 3).

Word Count

Menu Bar: Tools (Word Count)

Function Keys: Not Available

Description: Allows you to obtain the total word count of the current document.

Procedure:
1. Select Tools at any point in your document.
2. Click on Word Count.
3. WordPerfect counts and totals the words. When it is done, the total appears in a pop-up box, with a prompt to click on OK.

7

Lists and Macros

Lists and Macros are two very powerful WordPerfect features that are frequently ignored because they seem to be so complex. Lists (which include index, table of authorities, and table of contents entries) and Macros (which consist of keystrokes that you record for future use) are not so much difficult as they are tedious, with a number of steps to follow. However, once mastered, they can save you hours of time.

Indexes, tables of authorities, and tables of contents, while very different from one another, are each created the same way—by first coding the document for the entries that will be used, then defining the index or table, and finally generating the new table or index. This is a time-consuming activity, but it is not difficult. The key commands for these different kinds of lists are the Mark Text and the Master Document features.

Macros include repetitive keystrokes, such as some of those used in creating lists and tables of contents. My favorite macro is one that changes the font and the type size of a headline and then creates a table of contents entry. Instead of nine separate keystrokes, it requires only one (to the Button Bar).

Concordance

Menu Bar:	Not Available
Function Keys:	Not Available
Description:	Allows you to put frequently repeated words or phrases into a separate document that can be retrieved and merged when you generate

the index. This way, you do not have to mark each occurrence of the word or phrase in a document.

Procedure:
1. Type the frequently repeated words or phrases, ending each word or phrase with a hard return (<Enter>).

2. If you want subheads included with the words or phrases in the concordance file, you can make index entries in the concordance file. Otherwise, the word or phrase will serve as the index heading.

3. Save the file.

4. When defining the index, click on the Optional Concordance File box to enter the name of the file, including the pathname if the concordance file is not located in the same directory as the document being indexed.

Notes:
1. The Concordance feature is best used for long documents.

2. The problem with marking every occurrence of a word or phrase is that not every occurrence is significant; be careful which words you place in a concordance file.

See Also: *Index.*

Cross-Reference

Menu Bar:	Tools (Mark Text, Cross-Reference)
CUA Keyboard:	<F12>
WordPerfect 5.1 Keyboard:	<Alt><F5>

Description: Allows you to automatically create and update references (such as page or footnote numbers) in text.

**WordPerfect
Default:** Reference and Target, Page Number

Procedure: 1. Select Mark Text.

2. Decide whether you want to tag numbers (references), text (target), or both at the same time.

3. Choose the kind of reference that you want automatically updated.

4. Enter the target name (if you are only marking the reference or the text). Then click on OK, move the cursor to the desired location, and press <Enter>.

5. Repeat steps 1 through 4 throughout the document.

6. At the end of the document, create a page break (<Ctrl><Enter>) and then select Tools/Generate. You will have to generate the automatic references every time you want to update your document.

See Also: *Master Document; Footnotes/Endnotes* (Chapter 4).

Index

Menu Bar: Tools (Mark Text, Index)

**CUA
Keyboard:** <F12>

**WordPerfect
5.1 Keyboard:** <Alt><F5>

Description: Allows you to create an index of a single document or several documents.

WordPerfect
Default: No Concordance File

Procedure:

1. Create the index entry by moving the cursor to the word being indexed and select Tools. You can also block a phrase to index.

2. Choose Mark Text.

3. Click on Index.

4. A pop-up box appears with the word or highlighted phrase in the Heading box. To accept the word or phrase as the heading, click on the box to remove the highlight. To enter a different word or phrase as the heading, use the ‹←› key to remove the word and enter your own.

5. If you want a subheading with the index entry, click on the Subheading box. If you did not use the highlighted word or phrase, it appears here. To accept it, click on the box to remove the highlighting, or use the ‹←› key to remove the phrase and enter a different one.

6. Click on OK to save the changes and exit the Index box.

7. Repeat steps 1 through 6 for each word or phrase you want to index.

8. At the end of your file, insert a hard page break (‹Ctrl›‹Enter›) and select Tools/ Define.

9. Decide on the numbering style and click on it. If you have a concordance file, type in the name when prompted, including the pathname if the concordance file is

not in the same directory as the file you are indexing.

10. Click on OK and return to your document.

11. Save your file.

12. Return to the Tools Menu, this time selecting Generate.

13. A pop-up menu will appear, saying "Generate Updates all Lists, Indexes, ToCs, ToA, Cross-References, and Endnote Placement codes. Continue?" Click on Yes to generate the index.

Notes:

1. Postpone generating the index until you have marked and defined all your lists, such as the table of contents or the table of authorities.

2. If you have more than one file to index, use Master Documents to generate the index for the whole report. In this case, while you still create the index entries on the individual chapters, you do not define the index style or generate the index; that is done from Master Documents.

See Also:

Concordance, to put frequently repeated words or phrases into a separate file and avoid having to mark every occurrence of a word or phrase.

Mark Text; Marked Text, Define; Marked Text, Generate; Master Document.

_____ *Lists*

Menu Bar: Tools (Mark Text, List)

**CUA
Keyboard:** <F12>

**WordPerfect
5.1 Keyboard:** <Alt><F5>

Description: Allows you to create up to 10 separate lists.

Table 7.1. List Defaults

List	Purpose
List 1–5	User Defined
List 6	Figure Captions
List 7	Table Captions
List 8	Text Box
List 9	User Box
List 10	Equation Box

Procedure:

1. Highlight the text you want used in the list, and select Tools.

2. Choose Mark Text.

3. Click on List.

4. Enter the number of the list you want. Click on OK to save the changes and return to the document.

5. Repeat steps 1, 2, 3, and 4 until you complete the document. You can mark all the lists as well as the index, the table of contents, and the table of authorities at the same time, using different codes.

6. At the end of the document, create a page break (<Ctrl><Enter>) and select Tools/Define.

7. Click on List and choose the page number options for your first list. Click on OK to save the changes and return to the document.

8. If you are creating more than one list at a time, repeat step 6 until you have defined each list and numbering style.

9. Save your file.

10. Select Tools/Generate.

11. A pop-up menu will appear, saying "Generate Updates all Lists, Indexes, ToCs, ToA, Cross-References, and Endnote Placement codes. Continue?" Click on Yes to generate the list.

Notes:

1. If you have more than one related file to generate, use Master Documents; in this case, omit steps 5 through 9 for the individual documents.

2. Graphics captions, table box captions, text box captions, user-defined box captions, and equation captions do not need to be marked for inclusion. WordPerfect includes them automatically when they are created.

See Also: *Boxes (Table, Text, User)* (Chapter 9); *Mark Text; Marked Text, Define; Marked Text, Generate; Master Document.*

Macros, Assigning to Button Bar

Menu Bar: View (Button Bar Setup, Edit or New)

Function Keys: Not Available

Description: Allows you to assign most frequently used macros to the Button Bar for quicker access.

Procedure:

1. Select View.

2. Click on Edit (or New, to create a new Button Bar).

3. Click on Assigning Macro to Button. The macro directory appears.

4. If you always want the most recent version of the selected macro to be called when you press the Button Bar icon, ensure that

the Macro on Disk box at the bottom of the macro directory is checked. If you want a copy of the current macro saved to the Button Bar, make sure that the Macro on Disk box is not checked. In this case, the copy of the macro on the Button Bar will not be automatically updated when you update the macro.

5. Double-click on the macro you want added to the Button Bar. This puts the macro on the Button Bar and returns you to the Button Bar edit screen.

6. Make any other changes you want to the Button Bar, then click on OK to save the changes and return to your document.

Note: The above is the recommended procedure, but it does not always work. Instead, opening the Button Bar Edit Menu, then going to the Macro Menu to click on a macro from the assigned list sometimes has better results.

See Also: *Macros, Assigning to Macro Menu.*

Macros, Assigning to Macro Menu

Menu Bar: Macros (Assign to Menu)

Function Keys: Not Available

Description: Allows you to assign up to nine already-created macros to the Macro Menu for quicker access.

Procedure:
1. Select Macro at any point in your document.
2. Click on Assign to Macro.
3. Click on Insert.

4. Enter the name of the macro to be added to the Macro Menu, or use the button at the end of the box to select a file.

5. Use the mouse or the ⟨Tab⟩ key to go to the Text line and enter a brief description.

6. Repeat steps 4 and 5 to add other macros to the Macro Menu.

7. Click on OK to save the changes and return to the Macro Menu.

8. Click on OK to return to your document.

Macros, Converting

Menu Bar: File (File Manager, Run)

CUA Keyboard: Not Available

WordPerfect 5.1 Keyboard: ⟨F5⟩

Description: Allows you to convert macros from WordPerfect 5.1 for MS-DOS to WordPerfect 5.1 for Windows (within severe limits).

Procedure:

1. Select File Manager from a blank screen or at any point in any document. (This procedure has nothing to do with any currently-active document.)

2. Select File.

3. Choose Run.

4. Enter mfwin.exe in the filename box and click on Run.

5. Select Macro.

6. Choose Convert.

7. Move to the directory containing the macro to be converted and double-click on the desired file.

8. When the macro facility is through converting the macro, a message will be displayed telling you of any errors detected in the conversion. At this point you can convert another macro or press Cancel to return to the File Manager.

9. The new macro remains in its old directory. Use the Open (Move/Remove) command to put the macro in the WordPerfect for Windows macro directory.

Notes:

1. The new macro will have the same filename as before but a different extension; that is, a macro titled test. wpm in WordPerfect 5.1 is renamed test.wcm in WordPerfect for Windows.

2. The first time you call up the converted macro (or any macro that shipped with WordPerfect for Windows), the macro will be compiled, meaning that it will take a while to appear on your screen. The macros will not need to be compiled again unless you edit them.

3. You cannot convert macros that contain graphics (such as screens) from WordPerfect 5.1 to WordPerfect for Windows. The graphics just are not compatible. You can convert macros that are keystroke only, as long as the keys have not been assigned other functions.

4. Any keystrokes/commands that do not convert will be replaced with a comment and you will have to manually convert these keystrokes. Unconverted keystrokes/ commands will be bracketed with //,

meaning that WordPerfect will ignore
them. You will be able to see these ignored
commands when you view the file.

5. Always view or open a macro before using
it to be sure that it will perform as
expected.

See Also: *Macros, Recording.*

Macros, Playing

Menu Bar: Macro (Play)

**Function
Keys:**   <Alt><F10>

Description: Allows you play back an already-created
macro.

Procedure: 1. At the point in your document where you
want to use the macro, select Macro.

2. Click on Play. The macro menu will appear. The macro will play back the keystrokes you used when you created the
macro with the Macro Record. You cannot
modify the macro at this point.

3. Double-click on the macro you want.

See Also: *Macros, Recording.*

Macros, Recording

Menu Bar: Macro (Record)

**Function
Keys:**   <Ctrl><F10>

Description: Allows you to record keystrokes and duplicate
them for use at a later time. This includes

calling up style sheets (as long as the style sheet does not change its location in the Style Sheet Menu), inserting headers and footers, and using search and replace.

Procedure for Creating a Macro:

1. Select Macro at the point in your document where you are going to use the keystrokes in your macro.

2. Click on Record.

3. Give the macro a name.

4. Give a brief description. (This is optional.)

5. Type the keystrokes you want in the macro. If you need to stop in the middle of recording your macro to do something that is not part of the macro, use the Pause key. When you are ready to resume recording the macro, click on Pause again to continue the macro recording.

6. Click on the Macro/Stop Menu to end the macro recording.

Procedure for Editing a Macro:

1. Select File/Open.

2. Go to the Macro directory and double-click on the macro you want to edit.

3. Make your changes.

4. Select File/Save.

5. Select File/Close. The modified macro can now be used.

Notes:

1. You cannot use the Pause feature to record a pause into the macro. Pause is meant to allow you to temporarily interrupt your macro recording to do something else.

2. You can name your macros ^A-Z and ^0-9, just as you did in the MS-DOS 5.1 version

of WordPerfect. You can also name them
^<Shift>A-Z and ^<Shift>0-9. When
prompted to give the macro a name, enter
CTRL or CTRLSFT along with one character that is not already mapped on this keyboard; for example, a macro named
CTRLj.WCM can be started by pressing
<Ctrl>j.

See Also: *Macro, Assigning to Macro Menu; Macro,
Assigning to Button Bar; Macro, Playing.*

_____ *Mark Text*

Menu Bar: Tools (Mark Text)

**CUA
Keyboard:**   <F12>

**WordPerfect
5.1 Keyboard:**   <Alt><F5>

Description: Allows you to place hidden codes in text.
These codes can later be generated to create
lists of various sorts, tables of authorities and
contents, and indexes.

Procedure: 1. Highlight the text you want marked.

2. Select Tools.

3. Choose Mark Text.

4. Highlight the kind of entry you will later
want generated.

5. Answer the prompts about entry levels
and names.

6. Click on OK to save the changes and return to your document.

Notes:	1. You will need to mark every occurrence that you want listed, unless you create a concordance file.
	2. This is the first step in creating lists, tables of authorities and contents, and indexes. You must complete all three steps (mark, define, generate) to create the desired end result.
See Also:	*Concordance; Index; List; Marked Text, Define; Marked Text, Generate; Table of Authorities; Table of Contents.*

Marked Text, Define ———————————————

Menu Bar:	Tools (Define)
CUA Keyboard:	\<Shift>\<F12>
WordPerfect 5.1 Keyboard:	\<Alt>\<F5>
Description:	Allows you to define the lists and tables that you want generated.
Procedure:	1. At the point in your document where you want the list to appear, create a new page (\<Ctrl>\<Enter>).
	2. Select Tools.
	3. Choose Define.
	4. Click on the first list you want generated.
	5. Answer the prompts about levels and pagination.
	6. Click on OK to save the definition and return to your document.
	7. Repeat steps 2 through 6 for each list you want defined.

Note:	This is the second step in creating lists, tables of authorities and contents, and indexes. You must complete all three steps (mark, define, generate) to create the desired end result.
See Also:	*Index; Lists; Marked Text; Marked Text, Generate; Table of Authorities; Table of Contents.*

_____ *Marked Text, Generate*

Menu Bar:	Tools (Generate)
CUA Keyboard:	‹Alt›‹F12›
WordPerfect 5.1 Keyboard:	‹Alt›‹Shift›‹F5›
Procedure:	1. Save your file.
	2. At the point where you have defined your lists and tables, select Tools.
	3. Choose Generate.
	4. A pop-up menu will appear, saying "Generate Updates all Lists, Indexes, ToCs, ToA, Cross-References, and Endnote Placement codes. Continue?" Click on Yes to generate the lists. WordPerfect makes six passes through the document, searching for tables and lists. How long it takes to generate the document depends on the length of document and the speed of your computer.
Notes:	1. All of the defined sections will be generated in the order you defined them.
	2. If you have more than one related document to generate, use Master Documents; in this case, do not define the lists in the individual files.

3. This is the last step in creating lists, tables of authorities and contents, and indexes. You must complete all three steps (mark, define, generate) to create the desired end result.

Master Document _____

Menu Bar:	Tools (Mark Text, Master Document)
Function Keys:	Not Available
Description:	Allows you to combine a number of files into one easily managed file. Master Documents typically include a table of contents, codes for several files (called subdocuments), and an index. The subdocument codes can be replaced with the subdocuments themselves when you need to work with the whole report.

Procedure for Adding Subdocuments:

1. From a blank screen, select Tools.

2. Choose Master Document.

3. Click on Subdocument.

4. Double-click on the first file you want to link to others. A comment will be inserted on your screen that says "Subdoc: filename."

5. Repeat steps 2 through 4 for each document you want to link in this subdocument file.

6. Insert Mark Text definitions (such as those for a table of contents and an index) at the appropriate locations in the file (that is, insert the table of contents definition before subdocument one, and the index definition after the last subdocument).

7. Give the file a name and save it to the appropriate directory.

Procedure for Expanding or Condensing the Master Document:

1. Select Tools at any point in your subdocument file.

2. Choose Master Document.

3. Choose Expand Master or Condense Master.

4. If you choose Expand Master, WordPerfect automatically retrieves the text from each of the subdocuments into the Master Document file.

5. If you choose Condense Master, WordPerfect asks if you want to save the subdocuments before you delete them from the Master Document. Answer Yes if you made changes to the subdocuments, No if you made no changes to the subdocuments. The subdocuments are then saved to disk (or not), and the text is deleted from the Master Document. The subdocument codes remain in the subdocument file.

Notes:

1. You can generate a table of contents and index without expanding the subdocuments as long as the Mark Text definitions are in the file containing the subdocuments, and not in the subdocuments themselves.

2. Numbering, headers, and footers can be created in a Master Document just as they are in subdocuments. They will act the same way; that is, they will affect all text that comes after the Numbering or Header/Footer code. They will be superceded by any header or footer that is

placed after them in any of the subdocuments.

3. You can also print all the subdocuments in the Master Document without having to open each one.

See Also: *Lists; Headers/Footers* (Chapter 4); *Index; Table of Contents.*

Table of Authorities

Menu Bar: Tools (Mark Text, ToA Short Form or Full Form)

CUA Keyboard: <F12>

WordPerfect 5.1 Keyboard: <Alt><F5>

Description: Allows you to create a list of citations for a legal brief.

Procedure:
1. Block the text you want used in the table of authorities, and select Tools.

2. Choose Mark Text.

3. The highlighted text appears in the Short Form (nickname) box that will be used to label other occurrences of the same text. You can accept or change the Short Form and the section number. When the section number and Short Form name are correct, click on OK to edit the Full Form text.

4. Edit the text to make it appear as you want in the final form. Click on Close to save the edited text and return to your document.

5. Return to the beginning of the document.

6. Search (<F2>) for the next occurrence of this authority.

7. Select Tools/Mark Text/Short Form.

8. Enter the Short Form name.

9. Repeat steps 5, 6, 7, and 8 until you find every occurrence of the authority.

10. Repeat steps 1 through 9 for each citation you want listed.

11. At the place in your document where you want the section to appear, select Tools/Define.

12. Click on Table of Authorities, enter the section number, and change the format options as necessary.

13. Click on OK to save the changes and return to your document.

14. Repeat Steps 11 through 13 for each section you want defined.

15. Save your file.

16. Select Tools/Generate.

17. A pop-up menu will appear, saying "Generate Updates all Lists, Indexes, ToCs, ToA, Cross-References, and Endnote Placement codes. Continue?" Click on Yes to generate the table.

Notes:

1. All of the defined sections will be generated in the order you defined them.

2. If you have more than one related document to generate, use Master Documents; in this case, do not define the Table of Authorities in the individual files.

See Also: *Table of Contents.*

Table of Contents _____

Menu Bar:	Tools (Mark Text, Table of Contents)
CUA Keyboard:	<F12>
WordPerfect 5.1 Keyboard:	<Alt><F5>
Description:	Allows you to create a table of contents for a single document or several documents.

Procedure:

1. Create the table of contents entry by highlighting a word or phrase, and select Tools.

2. Choose Mark Text.

3. Click on Table of Contents.

4. Select a level number (1 through 5, with level 1 being flush left and level 5 being indented four times from the left margin).

5. Click on OK to save the change and return to your document.

6. Repeat steps 1 through 5 for each table of contents entry.

7. At the end of the document, insert a hard page break (<Ctrl><Enter>) and Select Tools/Define.

8. Choose the number of levels you want to include in the table of contents.

9. Choose the numbering style you want.

10. Click on OK to save the changes and return to your document.

11. Save your file.

12. Select Tools/Generate.

13. A pop-up menu will appear, saying "Generate Updates all Lists, Indexes, ToCs, ToA, Cross-References, and End-

note Placement codes. Continue?'' Click
on Yes to generate the table.

Note: If more than one file to will be used in the table of contents, use Master Document to gen-
erate the contents for the whole report. In
this case, while you still create the table of
contents entries in each file, you do not define the table of contents style or generate the
table of contents; that is done from Master
Document.

See Also: *Index; Lists; Master Document.*

8

Merge, Sort, and Labels

Merge, Sort, and Labels are some of WordPerfect's most feared features. However, while requiring a number of steps, these features are not difficult to use.

Merge allows you to take two files (such as a mass mailing letter and a list of addresses) and combine the information in them. Sort allows you to put lists in order, alphabetically or by whatever criteria you choose. You can sort any file, including secondary ones used in merges. Sort is frequently used in conjunction with Merge, and much of the terminology is the same for both features: for example, "records" refers to information being kept together, and "fields" refers to individual line items within a group.

Labels

Menu Bar:	Layout (Page, Paper Size)
CUA Keyboard:	\<Ctrl>\<F9>
Function Keys:	\<Shift>\<F8>
Description:	Allows you to create a label type and size to match the labels in your (WordPerfect or Windows-driven) printer.

Table 8.1. Add Paper Size Defaults

Paper Size Settings	Paper Size Defaults
Paper Type	Standard
Paper Size	Standard
Text Adjustments	Up 0"
	Right 0"
Paper Orientation	Portrait
Paper Location	Continuous
Paper Options	Double Sided Printing: Not Enabled
	Binding: Left

Procedure for Creating Labels Using WordPerfect Drivers:

1. Select Layout at any point on the page where you want the new size to take effect.
2. Choose Page.
3. Click on Paper Size.
4. Choose Add.
5. Modify the settings on the Add Paper Size screen.
6. Choose Labels.
7. Modify the settings on the screen as necessary for your labels.

Table 8.2. Add/Edit Label Screen Defaults

Label Settings	Label Defaults
Label Size	Width: 2.62 ˝
	Height: 1˝
Labels Per Page	Columns: 3
	Rows: 10
Top of Label	Top Edge: 0.500˝
	Left Edge: 0.187˝
Distance Between	Columns: 0/125
Labels	Rows: 0˝
Label Margins	Left: 0.112˝ (0.12˝, Windows)
	Right: 0.112˝ (0.22˝, Windows)
	Top/Bottom: 0˝

8. Click on OK to accept the new label settings and return to the Add Paper Size screen.

9. Click on OK to accept the Add Paper Size settings and return to the Paper Size screen.

10. The new setting is highlighted. Click on Select to choose the new setting for the current document.

Procedure for Creating Labels Using Windows Drivers:

1. Select Layout at any point on the page where you want the new size to take effect.

2. Choose Page.

3. Click on Paper Size.

4. Choose Add.

5. Click on OK when WordPerfect advises that you can only add label definitions when using Windows printer drivers.

6. Modify the settings on the Edit Labels screen as necessary for your labels.

7. Click on OK to accept the new label settings and return to the Paper Size screen.

8. The new setting is highlighted. Click on
Select to choose the new setting for the
current document. If you don't want the
new setting to take effect now, click on OK
to return to your document.

Notes:
1. You do not have to select the labels definition now. You can select it at any time after you have created the definition.

2. If you are working with the Merge feature
and labels, the label Paper Size codes must
be placed in Document Initial Codes (Lay-
out/Document/Initial Codes).

3. Refer to WordPerfect documentation for
detailed information on label sizes.

See Also: *Merge; Paper Size* (Chapter 4).

Chapter 11 for a brief discussion on the advantages and disadvantages of WordPerfect
and Windows printer drivers.

Merge

Menu Bar: Tools (Merge)

**CUA
Keyboard:** <Ctrl><F12>

**Function
Keys:** <Ctrl><F9>

Description: Allows you to combine two or more files having different data.

Procedure for Preparing the Secondary File:

1. Type the text of the file that will be
merged into the primary file (for example,
addresses that will be merged into a letter).

2. Divide the text into records by selecting Tools/Merge/End of Record at the end of each related group of information (such as after the name, address, salutation, and phone number).

3. Divide the records into fields by selecting Tools/Merge/End of Field at the end of each group of information that will always be merged at the same time. For example, a company name and address would be one field, and the name of an individual at that company would be another. You can have as many fields as you like, but each record must have the same number of fields, and each field must have the same kind of information; that is, if Field Two in one record has a company name, all Field Twos must have company names or nothing at all.

4. Add any other merge codes desired (use the Tools/Merge/Merge Codes Menu).

5. Save the file.

Procedure for Preparing the Primary File:

1. Type the text of the file.

2. Select Tools/Merge/Field at each point in the text where you want to insert material from the secondary file.

3. Repeat step 2 until you have completed inserting merge codes into the document.

4. Add any other merge codes desired (use the Tools/Merge/Merge Codes Menu).

5. Save the file.

Procedure for Merging the Two Files:

1. Select Tools on a blank screen.

2. Choose Merge.

3. Click on Merge.

4. Enter the name of the primary (text) file, including a pathname if the document is in another directory. (You can, alternatively, click on the button next to the Primary File box to go to the directory and double-click on the desired file.)

5. Enter the name of the secondary (address) file, including a pathname if the document is in another directory. (Alternatively, you can click on the button next to the Secondary File box to go to the directory and double-click on the desired file.)

6. The two files will be merged on your screen, allowing you to be sure the merge worked properly; that is, if your secondary file has 107 addresses, you will have 107 copies of the primary file with the merged information on your screen.

Note: All the Merge Codes that can be used in primary and secondary files are listed and can be accessed from the Tools/Merge/Merge Codes Menu.

See Also: *Labels; Macros* (Chapter 7); *Sort.*

Sort

Menu Bar:	Tools (Sort)
CUA Keyboard:	\<Ctrl>\<Shift>\<F12>
WordPerfect 5.1 Keyboard:	\<Ctrl>\<F9>
Description:	Allows you to sort lists by whatever criteria you choose.

Table 8.3. WordPerfect Sort Defaults

Sort Criteria	Sort Defaults
Record Type	Line
Sort Order	Ascending
Key Definitions	Key 1: Alphabetical, Field 1, Word 1

Procedure for Sorting a File:

1. Save the file to be sorted.
2. Select Tools at any point in your document.
3. Select Sort.
4. Change the settings to match the file; that is, if you want the file to sort alphanumerically on the first letter of the first word in the paragraph, change the options to reflect that.
5. When you are satisfied with the changes, click on OK to have the sort begin.

Procedure for Sorting a Block of Text:

1. Save the file to be sorted.
2. Block the text that you want sorted.
3. Select Tools.
4. Click on Sort.
5. Make the changes to reflect the sort criteria you want.
6. When you are satisfied with the changes, click on OK to sort the block. The sort overwrites the old block of text.

Note: Save your file before sorting, in case of problems with the sort.

See Also: *Merge.*

9

Graphics, Equations, Boxes, and Tables

"Graphics," in WordPerfect terminology, refers to figures, boxes, mathematical equations, and lines. The terminology used in graphics, equations, tables, and boxes is inextricably linked, although the functions themselves are far removed from one another.

Terms to be aware of:

Box	When WordPerfect refers to "Table Box," it is not suggesting that you create a table. Tables are created elsewhere. WordPerfect uses "box" classifications (table, text, user, and equations and figures) to make it easier to generate separate lists, such as in table of contents entries. What you are creating with a Table Box, Text Box, or User Box is a box around specified text.
Columns	This word, in WordPerfect, has two meanings. It can refer to a vertical column in a table, or to dividing a page into newspaper (vertical) or parallel (horizontal) columns. The uses are not interchangeable and are accessed through different commands.
Equation	WordPerfect performs no calculations in this mode. What WordPerfect does is help you format sophisticated equations. Whether the equation and its solution are accurate is up to you.

Mathematics   WordPerfect can perform some mathematical
                     functions in a table, acting almost like a
                     spreadsheet if you have set the table up
                     correctly.

Boxes (Table, Text, User)

Menu Bar: Graphics (Box, Create)

**Function
Keys:**   Not Available

Description: Allows you to either create or import an al-
                    ready-created table or other text into your
                    current document. Boxes created this way will
                    be numbered automatically according to their
                    type (for example, Table I, Text Box I, User
                    Box I), and the captions will also be generated
                    automatically when you generate the table of
                    contents and lists for your document.

Table 9.1. Table Box Defaults

Box Options	Defaults
Border Styles	Single (Table, Text)
	None (User)
Border Spacing	Table and Text Boxes
	Outside: 0.167″
	Inside: .0″
Gray Shading	10%
Caption Numbering	First Level: Numbers
	Second Level: Off
	Style: Bold
Caption Position	Below, Outside Box (Text, User)
	Above, Outside (Table)
Minimum Offset from Paragraph	0″

Procedure:
1. Select Graphics at the point in your document where you want the box to be placed.
2. Choose the Table Box you want.
3. Click on Options.
4. Change any of the default options (shown in Table 9.1).
5. Click on OK.
6. Select Graphics/Box/Create.
7. Click on the appropriate editor. If you are creating a text box, this step is skipped.
8. Enter the new text or go to the File/Retrieve Menu to bring an already-created file into the box.
9. Click on Box Position to move the box on the page (see Table 9.2).

Table 9.2. Table Box Position Defaults

Box Position	Defaults
Anchor To	Page
Number of Pages to Skip	0
Size	Auto Height Width: 3.25″
Vertical Position (on Page)	Set
Horizontal Position (on Page)	Set
Wrap Text Around Box	Enabled

10. Click on OK.
11. Click on Close to leave the editing box and return to your document.
12. If you want a caption, click on Graphics/Box/Caption to create one.

Notes:
1. To change the box specifications at a later time, choose the Graphic/Box/Edit option for the graphic you want to edit. This will

retrieve the selections you originally made for the box and allow you to change them.

2. To renumber the boxes beginning at any point, choose the Graphic/Box/New Number option at that point.

3. If you do not care about automatically generated captions, you may find it faster to create a box with the Table function.

See Also: *Tables.*

Columns, Newspaper or Parallel

See *Columns, Newspaper or Parallel* (Chapter 5).

Columns, Table

See *Tables*.

Equations

Menu Bar: Graphic (Equation, Create)

Function Keys: Not Available

Description: Allows you to create and insert mathematical equations and scientific formulas into a document.

Table 9.3.   Equation Box Defaults

Box Options	Defaults
Border Styles	None
Border Spacing	Outside: 0.083″
	Inside: .0″
Gray Shading	0%
Caption Numbering	First Level: Numbers
	Second Level: Off
	Style: Bold
Caption Position	Right
Minimum Offset from Paragraph	0″

Procedure: 1. Select the Graphics Menu at the point in your document where you want the equation to be positioned.

2. Choose Equation.

3. Click on Options to change the default settings shown in Table 9.3.

4. Make any changes and click on OK to return to your document.

5. Select Graphics/Equations/Create. This puts you in the Equation Editor.

Table 9.4.   Equation Box Position Defaults

Box Position	Defaults
Anchor To	Paragraph
Size	Auto Height
	Width: 6.5″
Vertical Position	0″
Horizontal Position	Margin, Full
Wrap Text Around Box	Enabled

6. Click on the Equ Position Button Bar icon to change the default position settings shown in Table 9.4. Click on OK to save

the changes and return to the Equation Editor.

7. Click on the Settings Button Bar icon to change some of the Equations Settings you established when setting up system defaults. (That is, you can change the graphic font size and the alignment. You cannot change the keyboard, though; you must return to the File/Preferences/Equations Menu to change your keyboard.)

8. Create your equation, or use the Retrieve Button Bar icon to import a previously created equation. Use the Redisplay Button Bar icon to see what the completed equation will look like.

9. Click on the Close Button Bar Icon to save your equation and return to your document.

Notes:

1. The equation editor palette contains several different screens with mathematical commands and symbols that allow you to create equations. It can only be used through the Equation Editor.

2. The font size of the equation is changed through the Settings Button Bar icon.

3. To change the box specifications or the equation itself at a later time, choose the Graphic/Equation/Edit option for the equation you want to edit. This will retrieve the selections you originally made for the box and allow you to change them.

See Also: *Equations* (Chapter 2), to change the keyboard.

Figure

Menu Bar:	Graphics (Figure, Create)
Function Keys:	Not Available
Description:	Allows you to use graphics provided with supported graphics packages in WordPerfect documents. Alternatively, the graphics can be produced in any package and converted into a format that is supported by WordPerfect.

Table 9.5.   Figure Box Defaults

Box Options	Defaults
Border Styles	Single
Border Spacing	Outside: 0.167″
	Inside: .0″
Gray Shading	0%
Caption Numbering	First Level: Numbers
	Second Level: Off
	Style: Bold
Caption Position	Below, Outside Box
Minimum Offset from Paragraph	0″

Procedure:	1. Select the Graphics Menu at the point in your document where you want the figure placed.
	2. Choose Figure.
	3. Choose Options to change the default settings shown in Table 9.5.
	4. Click on OK to return to your document.

To Retrieve a Graphic Without Making Any Changes:

1. Select Graphics/Figure/Retrieve.
2. The wpwin\Graphics Menu appears. Double-click on the desired graphic or change

directories to find the graphic you want.
The graphic you selected appears on your
screen at the position you indicated.

3. If you want a caption, select Graphics/Fig-
   ure/Caption to create a heading for your
   document.

Table 9.6.   Figure Box Position Defaults

Box Position	Defaults
Anchor To	Page
Number of Pages to Skip	0
Size	Auto Height Width: 3.25″
Vertical Position (On Page)	Set
Horizontal Position (On Page)	Set
Wrap Text Around Box	Enabled

To Retrieve a Graphic to Modify:

1. Select Graphics/Figure/Create to retrieve a
   graphic and modify it. (You cannot create
   graphics from scratch in WordPerfect, but
   you can change orientation and size.)

2. The Graphics Editor window appears.

   a. Click on the Figure Pos Button Bar
      icon if you want to change any of the
      defaults shown in Table 9.6.

   b. Click on Retrieve to go to the
      wpwin\Graphics Menu. Double-click
      on the desired graphic or change di-
      rectories to find the graphic you want.

   c. The graphic appears on the Graphics
      Editor screen. Make any orientation
      and sizing changes necessary.

   d. When you are through modifying the
      graphic, click on the Close Button Bar
      icon to save the changes and return to

your document. (To exit without saving, select the File/Cancel Menu.)

3. If you want a caption, select Graphics/Figure/Caption to create a heading for your graphic.)

Notes:

1. If you are going to use the graphic more than once in your document, or if you are concerned about the amount of memory the graphic will take when stored with your document, use the Graphic on Disk in the File Menu.

2. To change the figure specifications at a later time, choose the Graphic/Figure/Edit option for the figure you want to edit. This will retrieve the selections you originally made for the figure and allow you to change them.

3. To renumber the figures beginning at any point, choose the Graphic/Figure/New Number option at that point.

4. Graphics formats supported by Word-Perfect include:

.CGM	.DHP	.DXF
.EPS	.GEM	.HPGL
.IMG	.MSP	.PCX
.PIC	.PNTG	.PPIC
.TIFF	.WMF	.WPG
.BMP (Windows 3.0 or later)		

_____ *Line Draw*

Menu Bar:	Tools (Line Draw)
Function Keys:	<Ctrl>D

Description: Allows you to draw a horizontal or vertical line in your document, or a box around text.

Procedure:
1. Select Line Draw at the point in your document where you want the line or box drawn.
2. Highlight the character you want to use for Line Draw, or click on Character to select your own.
3. Use the left-, right-, up-, or down-arrow keys to draw your line or box. Remember that WordPerfect is in Typeover Mode now, meaning that any text in the path of the Line Draw will be erased, not pushed out of the way.
4. Erase mistakes by clicking on Erase and then going back over your mistake. (This does not restore deleted text.)
5. Click on Move to move the Line Draw cursor without creating a line.
6. Click on Close to leave Line Draw and return to your document. WordPerfect also leaves the Typeover Mode at this time, unless you were using it outside of Line Draw.

Notes:
1. You must use a monospaced font (nonproportional) in order for the lines to print correctly. Even then, the quality of the printed line depends in very large part on the capabilities of your printer.
2. Line Draw is an old WordPerfect feature that is still available so that WordPerfect for Windows can support older documents that use this command. WordPerfect now has other, more efficient features that can do the same thing as Line Draw.

See Also: *Boxes (Table, Text, User); Line, Graphic.*

Line, Graphic

Menu Bar: Graphics (Line, Create Horizontal, or Create Vertical)

**CUA
Keyboard:** <Ctrl><F11>

**WordPerfect
5.1 Keyboard:** <Alt><F9>

Description: Allows you to draw a horizontal or vertical line in your document.

Table 9.7. Graphic Line Defaults

Horizontal/Vertical Line	Defaults
Length	Change through Vertical/ Horizontal Position
Thickness	.013″
Gray Shading	100%
Vertical Position	Baseline (Horizontal) Full Page (Vertical)
Horizontal Position	Full Page (Horizontal) Left Margin (Vertical)

Procedure:
1. Select the Graphics Menu at the point in your document where you want the line drawn.
2. Choose Line.
3. Click on Horizontal or Vertical.
4. Change the default settings (shown in Table 9.7) to your needs. You can specify the Vertical/Horizontal Position settings if the preset options are not satisfactory.
5. Click on OK to activate the line and return to your document.

Note: The line does not show up on the page except as a code that is visible in Reveal Codes.

You only can see the line itself when using Print Preview.

See Also: *Boxes (Table, Text, User).*

Line Draw, to draw a line that is visible at all times on the screen.

Print Preview (Chapter 11); *Tables.*

Math

See *Tables, Math.*

Rows, Table

See *Tables.*

Tables

Menu Bar:	Layout (Tables)
CUA Keyboard:	<Ctrl><F9>
WordPerfect 5.1 Keyboard:	<Alt><F7>
Description:	Allows you to enter rows and columns of data without tabs.

Table 9.8.   Table Option Defaults

Options	Default
Columns/Rows	The number you selected
Cell Margins	.083″ all around
Shading	10%
Position (on Page)	Left Margin
Negative Result Display	Minus Sign
Header Rows	0
Disable Cell Locks	No

Procedure:
1. Select Layout.
2. Choose Tables.
3. Click on Create.
4. Enter the number of columns (vertical) and rows (horizontal) that you want in the table. The table is created, and you are returned to your document.
5. Select Layout/Tables/Options to change the setting defaults (shown in Table 9.8).
6. Format the individual rows through the Cell, Column, Row, and Lines selection on the Layout/Tables Menu.
7. Enter the data into your table, using the <Tab> key to get from cell to cell and the Center command to center text in the cell.

Note: You can customize a table by highlighting the individual cells and clicking on Layout/Tables/Join or Split. You can also add or delete columns or rows by moving the cursor to a row or column and clicking on Layout/Tables/Insert or Delete.

Shortcut: Click and drag on the Ruler Bar Table Grid (under the Macro Menu).

See Also: *Boxes; Line Draw; Line, Graphics; Tables, Math.*

Tables, Math

Menu Bar:	Layout (Tables)
CUA Keyboard:	\<Ctrl>\<F9>
WordPerfect 5.1 Keyboard:	\<Alt>\<F7>
Description:	Allows you to perform four-function math in a table.
Procedure:	1. Select Layout while the cursor is in the table cell where you want the results displayed.
	2. Choose Tables.
	3. Click on Formula to perform basic math functions (cell A1 times cell B1, for example). As soon as you enter the formula and click on OK to return to the screen, the total is entered in the table. (Calculate is used if you have changed table data in a way that affects the calculations previously made.)
Note:	To be recognized as math functions, +, =, and * must be entered while you are in Layout/Tables/Formula. (The plus sign serves as a subtotal function, the equal sign as a total, and the asterisk as a grand total.) If you create them outside of Formula, they will not be recognized as math.

10

Spreadsheets

WordPerfect does not, itself, allow you to create spreadsheets. However, you can bring a spreadsheet into an existing WordPerfect document and edit it. WordPerfect supports several spreadsheet packages, among them Lotus 1-2-3, Microsoft Excel, Quattro and Quattro Pro, and, of course, PlanPerfect, its own spreadsheet package. Be aware that WordPerfect's Spreadsheet feature does not support all versions of these applications.

Terms to be aware of:

DDE Link   WordPerfect lets you create a link between a
               WordPerfect document and any file created by
               a Windows application that also supports Dy-
               namic Data Exchange (DDE). A DDE file can
               be of any type (text, graphs, tables, and the
               like), and it is not limited to spreadsheets.
               This link is accessed through the Edit (Link)
               Menu.

Link   WordPerfect can create a link between a
               spreadsheet from a supported application (see
               above) and a WordPerfect document. No
               other type of file can be imported through the
               spreadsheet link. This link is accessed through
               the Tools (Spreadsheet) Menu.

DDE Link

Menu Bar: Edit (Link)

**Function
Keys:**   Not Available

Description: Allows you to link a file created by a Windows application to a WordPerfect document.

Procedure to Link Two Documents that Are Each Open:

1. Switch to the DDE document and copy to the Clipboard the data to be linked.

2. Return to the WordPerfect document and place the cursor at the point where you want the linked text to be inserted.

3. Select Edit.

4. Choose Link.

5. Click on Paste Link. A copy of the data is placed in your file, and the data is linked to the original DDE document. (If Paste Link is dimmed, your DDE application will not let you link the two files. Refer to the documentation that came with your DDE application.)

Procedure to Link Two Documents Without Opening the Source Document:

1. Select Edit at the point where you want the linked text to be inserted.

2. Choose Link.

3. Click on Create.

4. Enter the application, file, and item names in the Source File and Item box. The link codes are placed in your WordPerfect document, but the linked data will not be copied or updated until both files are open. If the WordPerfect document is opened first, you will have to use the Update Link Dialog Box; the linked data will not be automatically updated.

5. Enter a name for the link in the Link Name box, which identifies this link in the DDE codes in your document.

6. Click on Automatic or Manual to change the updating method (automatic is the default); click on Text or Graphics if you want to change the storage method (Text is the default).

7. Click on OK to insert the link and return to your document.

Note: Not all Windows applications support DDE. WordPerfect can link files only from those applications that support DDE.

See Also: *Convert from Other Format* (Chapter 3); *Spreadsheet, Link.*

Spreadsheet, Import

Menu Bar: Tools (Spreadsheet, Import)

Function Keys: Not Available

Description: Allows you to bring a spreadsheet into a WordPerfect document and format and edit it.

Procedure:
1. Select Tools.
2. Choose Spreadsheet.
3. Choose Import.
4. Enter the filename of the spreadsheet.
5. Choose Range.
6. Enter the range (or block) of cells you want to import. (The default is the whole spreadsheet.)
7. Choose Type if you want to import the spreadsheet as WordPerfect text instead of as a table.
8. Click on OK. The document will now be imported into the WordPerfect document.

Note: Import is used when the spreadsheet will not
need to be updated. If the spreadsheet needs
to be updated, use the Link option instead.

See Also: *Boxes (Table, Text, User)* (Chapter 9); *Spreadsheet, Link.*

Spreadsheet, Link _____

Menu Bar: Tools (Spreadsheet, Create Link)

**Function
Keys:**   Not Available

Description: Allows you to import a spreadsheet into a
WordPerfect document. With the link option,
the spreadsheet can first be modified in the
spreadsheet package and then automatically
updated in the WordPerfect document.

Procedure: 1. Select Tools.

2. Choose Spreadsheet.

3. Click on Create Link.

4. Enter the filename of the spreadsheet.

5. Choose Range.

6. Enter the range (or block) of cells you
want to link to your WordPerfect document. (The default is the whole
spreadsheet.)

7. Choose Type if you want to import the
spreadsheet as WordPerfect text instead of
as a table.

8. Click on OK. The spreadsheet will now be
imported into the WordPerfect document.

Notes: 1. If you format or edit a linked spreadsheet,
the changes will be lost the next time you
update the link.

2. If you want the spreadsheet to be updated every time it is retrieved by WordPerfect, you must modify the Link options to permit this.

See Also: *DDE Link; Spreadsheet, Import; Spreadsheet, Link Options.*

_____ *Spreadsheet, Link Options*

Menu Bar: Tools (Spreadsheet, Link Options)

Function Keys: Not Available

Description: Allows you to change the default options for importing a spreadsheet in Link mode.

Procedure:
1. Select Tools.
2. Choose Spreadsheet.
3. Click on Link Options.
   a. If you want current spreadsheet data to be retrieved whenever you call up the WordPerfect document that contains the spreadsheet, click on the Update on Retrieve option.
   b. If you do not want the Link codes visible on the screen (they show the beginning and end of the imported document), click on the Show Link Codes option to toggle it off. (The default is On.)
4. When you are satisfied with the changes, click on OK to save the changes and return to your document.

Notes: WordPerfect can only retrieve the last-saved information. If new information has been entered into the spreadsheet, the spreadsheet must be saved to disk before the WordPerfect document containing the spreadsheet is retrieved.

See Also: *Spreadsheet, Import; Spreadsheet, Link.*

11

Printing

You have many printing options with this version of Word-Perfect. For one thing, WordPerfect has many typesetting capabilities and can position text and graphics on a page more precisely than ever before. Also, you can print through WordPerfect or through the Windows application.

Several advantages exist for using WordPerfect printer drivers rather than following Windows tradition and using Windows printer drivers.

- You can adjust the quality of text and graphics individually. Changing the print quality settings in WordPerfect may have no effect on some Windows printer drivers.

- You can print your document more quickly.

- You are not limited to one paper size throughout your document, and you have great flexibility to change and edit paper definitions.

- WordPerfect for Windows printer drivers are compatible with printer drivers from the MSDOS version of Word-Perfect, and, if you have not changed printers, no reformatting is required.

- WordPerfect printer features may not translate to Windows; that is, you do not have the same flexibility or number of formatting choices as with a WordPerfect printer driver, you cannot add or modify a Windows printer driver or Windows cartridges/fonts through the WordPerfect printer program, and you cannot print to disk the same way.

On the other hand, several reasons exist to use a Windows printer driver:

- If you select a system font, your document will be formatted with the same font regardless of the printer you are using.

• If the printer and the Windows printer driver support color, you can print any color graphics you have included in your document.

Refer to Appendix A to install and use Windows printer drivers.

Adding Printer

See *Printer, Selecting.*

Advance

Menu Bar:	Layout (Advance)
CUA Keyboard:	Not Available
WordPerfect 5.1 Keyboard:	\<Shift>\<F8>
Description:	Allows you to position text a specified distance from the current printing position, or at a specified position on the page.
Procedure:	1. Select Layout at the spot you want to move the text.
	2. Choose Advance.
	3. A box with positioning alternatives appears. Click on the option you want, then type in the distance desired.
	4. Click on OK to return to your document.

To Return to the Original Printing Position:

1. Move the cursor to the end of the text you want printed in an Advance position.

2. Select Layout/Advance.

3. Reverse the choices you made earlier; that is, if you advanced up by one inch, advance down by one inch.

4. Click on OK to your document.

Note: This command is not meant as a substitute for superscript or subscript text. It is designed to position a block of text precisely, somewhere other than where the printer thinks the text belongs.

See Also: *Center Line* (Chapter 5); *Center Page; Font Attributes* (Chapter 5).

_____ *Binding Offset*

See *Print.*

_____ *Block, Printing*

See *Print, Block.*

_____ *Cancel Print Job*

Menu Bar: Not Available

Function Keys: Not Available

Description: Allows you to remove the current print job from the print queue. It has no effect on previously sent print jobs.

Figure 11.1.   Current Print Job Dialog Box

```
┌──────────────────────────────────────────┐
│              Current Print Job             │
│               Print Status                 │
│                                            │
│  Status:                                   │
│  Page Number:                              │
│  Current Copy:                             │
│  Message:                                  │
│  Action:                                   │
│                        Cancel Print Job    │
└──────────────────────────────────────────┘
```

Procedure: 1. When the current print job is printing, the Current Print Job Dialog Box appears on your screen. If you want to cancel the job, click on Cancel Print Job.

2. When the dialog box disappears, the Current Print Job has already been sent to the printer and you can no longer stop the print job through WordPerfect. Other ways to stop the print job are through the printer (take the printer off line and reset it) or through the Windows Print Manager (refer to Appendix A).

Cartridges and Soft Fonts

Menu Bar: File (Select Printer, Setup)

Function Keys: Not Available

Description: Allows you to change fonts with print cartridges, print wheels, or downloadable font files.

Procedure: 1. Select File.

2. Choose Select Printer.

3. Choose Setup.

4. Click on Cartridges and Fonts.

5. Highlight the kind of fonts you want to add. Click on Select to go to the font list.

6. Decide whether you want the soft fonts to be always available or available only for particular print jobs. Then click on Present When Print Job Begins or Can Be Loaded/Unloaded During Job.

7. Highlight fonts to add them to the active list. Each active font is marked with an asterisk or a plus sign, depending on which method you chose in step 6.

8. Click on OK to save the changes and return to the Cartridges and Fonts screen.

9. Click on Close to return to the Setup screen.

10. Move the cursor to Path for Downloadable Fonts and Printer Commands and specify the font location (pathname) so that WordPerfect can locate the soft fonts when it needs them.

11. Click on OK to save the changes and return to the Select Printer screen.

12. Click on Close to return to your document.

Note: If you told WordPerfect that the fonts will be present when the print job begins, you will need to initialize the printer prior to the print job. At that point, the fonts marked with a plus sign will be downloaded to the printer. If you used the plus sign to mark fonts, you do not need to initialize the printer. In either case, do not mark fonts that you do not have. WordPerfect cannot create fonts.

See Also: *Initialize Printer.*

Center Page

Menu Bar:	Layout (Page, Center Page)
CUA Keyboard:	\<Alt\>\<F9\>
WordPerfect 5.1 Keyboard:	\<Shift\>\<F8\>
Description:	Allows you to center a page top-to-bottom for the printer. The page will not be centered on your monitor screen but it will show up at the Printer Preview.

Procedure: 1. Move to the beginning of the page you want centered.

2. Select Layout.

3. Choose Page.

4. Click on Center Page. The page is now centered, as indicated by the check mark next to the Center Page option in the Layout/Page Menu. To turn off the toggle, click on it again.

Note: Make sure that the Center Page code comes first in the codes on the page, or the page will not center. Do not center a page with footnotes or endnotes.

Color Printing

Menu Bar:	Font (Color)

Function Keys:	Not Available

Description: Allows you, if you have a color printer, to select the color of the printed text.

Procedure:

1. Select Font at the point in your document where you want the type to be a different color.

2. Choose Color.

3. Choose a color by selecting a predefined color, or make up your own color by editing an existing print color in Color Options.

4. Click on OK to save the changes and return to your document.

5. At this point, an informational message appears, telling you the color changes will not show up if you are using Windows System colors. Click on OK.

6. Move the cursor to the point where you want the type to revert to the original color.

7. Choose Font/Color.

8. Return the color settings to their original settings.

9. Click on OK to save the changes and return to your document.

See Also: *Display* (Chapter 2) to disable Windows System colors.

Document on Disk, Printing from

Menu Bar: File (Print, Document on Disk)

CUA
Keyboard: ⟨F5⟩

WordPerfect
5.1 Keyboard: ⟨Shift⟩⟨F7⟩

Description: Allows you to print part or all of a document
                   without first retrieving it to the screen.

Procedure: 1. Select File at any point in your document.

                   2. Choose Print.

                   3. Choose Document on Disk.

                   4. Click on Print.

                   5. Enter the name of the file, including a
                      complete pathname if the file is not in the
                      default directory, or click on the icon next
                      to the Filename box to select the document
                      you want printed.

                   6. You can print all the pages (the default), or
                      you can print selected pages by typing
                      specific page numbers with commas but no
                      spaces (1,2,4,6,7) or as a range (15–20).

                   7. Click on Print to begin printing and return
                      to your document.

Note: You will not be able to do anything on your
                   screen until the print job is sent to the printer.

See Also: *Multiple Pages, Printing; Print.*

Font, Choosing

Menu Bar: File (Print, Select Printer)

Function
Keys: Not Available

Description: Allows you to choose a default printer font
                   for the document.

Procedure:	1. Select File at any point in the document.
	2. Choose Select Printer.
	3. Choose Setup.
	4. Choose Initial Font.
	5. All the fonts supported by the currently selected printer will appear on the screen. Highlight the desired font.
	6. Highlight a point size.
	7. Click on OK to save the changes and return to the Printer Setup Dialog Box. Click on OK to return to the Select Printer Dialog Box.
	8. Click on Close to return to your document.
Note:	The font change will not affect any currently existing document unless you also change the initial font for that document. However, all new documents will have the new font as the default.
See Also:	*Font, Initial* (Chapter 5) to change the typeface for currently existing documents.

Fonts, Automatic Font Changes

See *WordPerfect Printer Drivers, Modifying.*

Fonts, Soft

See *Cartridges and Soft Fonts.*

Fonts, Substituting

See *WordPerfect Printer Drivers, Modifying.*

Forms, Printing _____

Menu Bar:	Layout (Page, Paper Size)
CUA Keyboard:	⟨Alt⟩⟨F9⟩
WordPerfect 5.1 Keyboard:	⟨Shift⟩⟨F8⟩
Description:	Allows you to print forms.
Procedure:	1. Select Layout at any point in your document.
	2. Choose Page.
	3. Click on Paper Size.
	4. Highlight the forms paper type you created earlier.
	5. Click on Select.
	6. Select File.
	7. Choose Print and click on the printing parameters you want.
	8. Click on Print to print your document.
See Also:	*Print; Paper Size* (Chapter 4).
	See *Forms* (Chapter 4) to create a unique form definition.

Full Document, Printing _____

See *Print.*

Graphics, Quality _____

See *Print.*

Initialize Printer

Menu Bar:	File (Print, Initialize Printer)
CUA Keyboard:	<F5>
WordPerfect 5.1 Keyboard:	<Shift><F7>
Description:	Allows you to download cartridges and fonts to the printer.
Procedure:	1. Select File when you are ready to print the document that will require the downloaded fonts/cartridges.
	2. Choose Print.
	3. Click on Initialize Printer.
	4. WordPerfect will ask: "Proceed with Printer Initialization?" Click on Yes. WordPerfect will then download to the printer the fonts marked with an asterisk on the Setup Printer Menu.
See Also:	*Cartridges and Soft Fonts.*

Landscape Printing

Menu Bar:	Layout (Page, Paper Size)
CUA Keyboard:	<Alt><F9>
WordPerfect 5.1 Keyboard:	<Shift><F8>
Description:	Allows you to print with a landscape orientation. This command will not work if your printer does not support landscape printing.

Procedure: 1. Select Layout at the page in your document where you want landscape printing to begin.

2. Choose Page.

3. Click on Paper Size.

4. Select the landscape paper type.

5. Select File.

6. Choose Print and click on the printing parameters you want.

7. Click on Print to print your document.

Notes: 1. Select Landscape before you create your document because the different page forces new margins.

2. The Landscape page code positions itself at the top of the page where you selected it and takes effect from that point forward.

See Also: *Print.*

Paper Size (Chapter 4) to create a landscape paper definition; *Environment, Changing* (Chapter 2) to disable the auto page code.

Multiple Files, Printing ─────────────────────

Menu Bar: File (File Manager)

**CUA
Keyboard:**   Not Available

**WordPerfect
5.1 Keyboard:**   ⟨F5⟩

Description: Allows you to print multiple files without having to open each one first.

Procedure: 1. Choose File at any point in your document.

2. Use the Navigator to go to the directory where the multiple files to be printed are located.

3. Click and drag with the mouse to highlight the files you want printed, or click on the Edit/Select All Menu Bar. If the files are scattered in the directory, or over several directories, you will have to print them in groups.

4. Click on File/Print to print the multiple documents.

5. A dialog box will appear, prompting you to print or cancel. Click on Print to print the files. You will automatically be returned to your document.

Note: WordPerfect is not a multitasking application. You will not be able to work on anything else until all of the jobs have been sent to the printer.

See Also: *File Manager Navigator* (Chapter 3).

Print Manager if you receive a Can't Open Printer Device error message.

Multiple Pages, Printing

Menu Bar: File (Print, Multiple Pages)

CUA Keyboard: <F5>

WordPerfect 5.1 Keyboard: <Shift><F7>

Description: Allows you to print specific pages of a document rather than the whole document.

WordPerfect Default: Print All

Procedure:	1. Select File.
	2. Choose Print.
	3. Choose Multiple Pages.
	4. Click on Print.
	5. Enter the range of pages you want printed. Either type in the actual numbers with commas but no spaces (for example, 1,3,4,6,7) or type a range (for example, 15–20).
	6. Click on Print to begin printing and return to your document.

Page, Printing

See *Print*.

Page Size and Type, Choose

See *Page Size* (Chapter 4).

Print

Menu Bar:	File (Print)
CUA Keyboard:	⟨F5⟩
WordPerfect 5.1 Keyboard:	⟨Shift⟩⟨F7⟩
Description:	Allows you to print all or part of a document and to change the number of copies and document settings.

Table 11.1. Printer Default Settings

Print	
Current Printer	Your selection
Default Print Setting	Full document

Copies	
Number of Copies	1
Generated By	WordPerfect

Document Settings	
Binding Offset	0"
Graphics Quality	Medium
Text Quality	High

Procedure: 1. Select File when you are ready to print your document.

2. Choose Print.

3. If you want to print something other than the full document, click on the desired option.

4. Change the Copies and Document settings as necessary.

5. Click on Print. The Print Job Status Box will appear.

6. As soon as the entire job has been sent to the printer, you will be returned to your document. If you want to cancel the job at this point, click on Cancel Print Job.

Shortcut: <Ctrl>P, as long as you want to print the entire document. (You do not have the opportunity to change any settings with this command; it prints everything.)

See Also: *Cancel Print Job; Document on Disk, Printing from; Initialize Printer; Multiple Files, Printing; Multiple Pages, Printing; Printer,*

Initial Settings (Chapter 2); *Printer, Selecting; Print to Disk.*

Print, Block

Menu Bar:	File (Print)
CUA Keyboard:	⟨F5⟩
WordPerfect 5.1 Keyboard:	⟨Shift⟩⟨F7⟩
Description:	Allows you to print selected text.
Procedure:	1. Highlight the text you want printed.
	2. Select File.
	3. Choose Print. The Options box will appear, with Selected Text already highlighted.
	4. Make any changes desired in the Print Dialog Box.
	5. Click on Print. The Print Job Status Dialog Box will appear on your screen while the job is being sent to the printer.
Note:	Your highlighted text will be printed in the same page position it had in your document. That is, if you highlighted the last three lines of one page and the first two of the next, the five highlighted lines (and any headers and footers) will be printed on two separate pages that are otherwise very nearly blank.

Print, Color

See *Color Printing.*

_____ *Print, Double Sided*

Menu Bar: Layout (Page, Paper Size)

**CUA
Keyboard:**   <Alt><F9>

**WordPerfect
5.1 Keyboard:**   <Shift><F8>

Description: Allows you to choose a paper definition for double-sided documents. Your printer must be capable of duplex printing for this option to take effect.

Procedure:
1. Select Layout at any point in your document.
2. Choose Page.
3. Click on Paper Size.
4. Click on Add.
5. Scroll through the list of paper types to create a unique paper type. (Unique means that you do not have it listed already in the paper sizes you have defined.)
6. Click on Double-Sided Printing to turn the option on.
7. Change the Binding setting if necessary.
8. Click on OK to save the changes and return to the Paper Size window.
9. Click on Select to choose the new definition.
10. Select File.
11. Choose Print, and click on the printing parameters you want.
12. Click on Print to print your document.

See Also: *Print.*

Print, Full Document

See *Print*.

Print, Graphics

See *Print*.

Print, Page

See *Print*.

Print, Selected Pages

See *Multiple Pages, Printing*.

Print Job, Cancel

See *Cancel Print Job*.

Print Manager

Menu Bar:	Not Available
Function Keys:	Not Available
Description:	Allows you to enable or disable the Windows Print Manager in response to your printing needs.
Procedure:	1. Click on the single down arrow in the extreme upper right-hand corner of the WordPerfect window.
	2. Double-click on the Windows Main Menu.

3. Double-click on Control Panel.

4. Double-click on Printers.

5. Click on the Print Manager box at the bottom of the screen to change the toggle from On to Off, or vice versa.

6. Click on OK to save the change and return to the Control Panel window.

7. Double-click on the Control Menu Box (at the upper left-hand corner of the Control Panel window) to close the window and return to the Main Menu window.

8. Double-click on the Control Menu Box again to close the Main Menu window.

9. Your document should be on the desktop, with the WP logo. Double-click on the WP logo to restore your document to the screen

Note: Use this function when you receive the error message "Can't Open Printer Device."

See Also: Appendix A, **WordPerfect and Windows.**

_____ *Print Multiple Files*

See *Multiple Files, Printing.*

_____ *Print Multiple Pages*

See *Multiple Pages, Printing.*

_____ *Print Preview*

Menu Bar: File (Print Preview)

CUA
Keyboard: <Shift><F5>

WordPerfect
5.1 Keyboard: <Shift><F7>

Description: Allows you to view a document, including headers, footers, type size, and graphics, just as the document will appear when it is printed. You cannot edit the document while in Print Preview.

Procedure: 1. Select File at the page you want to preview.

2. Click on Print Preview.

3. "Please Wait" will appear on the screen as WordPerfect formats and shows you the document.

4. The Print Preview Button Bar appears on the left-hand side of your screen, allowing you to zoom in on a particular section of the page you are previewing or to quickly look at the previous or the following page, or at facing pages.

5. When you have finished viewing your document, click on Close to return to your document. You will return to the page that you were last viewing, not the page where you entered Print Preview.

Print Quality, Graphics _____

See *Print.*

Print Qualtiy, Text _____

See *Print.*

Print to Disk

Menu Bar:	File (Print, Select Printer)
CUA Keyboard:	<F5>
WordPerfect 5.1 Keyboard:	<Shift><F7>
Description:	Allows you to print your document to a disk rather than a printer.

Procedure:

1. Select File at any point in your document.
2. Choose Print.
3. Choose Select.
4. Click on Setup.
5. Use the mouse at the Destination/Port box to click and drag to File.
6. Enter a name for the document to be printed to, including a pathname if the disk is not the default directory (for example, A:\test).
7. Click on OK to save the changes and return to the Select Printer screen; click on Close to return to the Print screen.
8. Click on Print to print the document to the filename instead of the printer.

Note: Reverse the steps to change the Destination/Port setting back to its default when you have finished the print job. This setting will otherwise be in effect until you change it, and all succeeding documents will print over the original printed file instead of being printed to a printer.

Printer Commands

Menu Bar: Layout (Typesetting)

**Function
Keys:**   Not Available

Description: Allows you to add commands to your document in order to take advantage of the special features of your printer.

Table 11.2.   WordPerfect Typesetting Commands

Typesetting Defaults	
Word Spacing	WordPerfect Optimal
Letterspacing	WordPerfect Optimal
Word Spacing	Compressed to 60%
Justification Limits	Expanded to 400%
Line Height Adjustment	Between Lines: 0″
	Between Paragraphs: 0″
Underline	Underline Spaces
Kerning	Off
First Baseline at Top Margin	Off
Printer Command	Off

Procedure: 1. Select Layout at the point in your document where you want to add the special printer feature.

2. Click on Typesetting.

3. The Typesetting Dialog Box will appear.

    a. Change the defaults as required.

    b. If you have a special command for the printer, click on Printer Command and enter the command for the special printer feature. Click on OK to return to the Typesetting Dialog Box.

4. Click on OK to save the changes and return to your document.

Notes: 1. Refer to your printer manual for commands that can be used in your document. Remember that WordPerfect can handle most situations without need of printer commands.

2. Printer commands are only displayed in Reveal Codes. You will not see them on the screen otherwise.

3. You cannot use these typesetting commands if you are using Windows printer drivers.

Printer, Deleting

Menu: File (Select Printer)

Function Keys: Not Available

Description: Allows you to remove a printer from the Printer Select screen.

Procedure: 1. Select File at any point in your document.

2. Choose Select Printer.

3. Highlight the printer you wish to remove from the printer list.

4. Click on Delete.

5. A message appears, asking you to confirm that you want that printer's driver removed. Click on OK. The printer disappears from the list.

6. Click on Close to return to your document.

Note: Documents that were originally created with the now deleted printer will still try to print with it. Since the driver is no longer there, the printing will not be satisfactory. You will have to manually select a different printer for

each document that was created with the old
driver.

Printer Drivers _____

See *WordPerfect Printer Drivers.*

Printer, Initializing _____

See *Initialize Printer.*

Printer, Installing _____

Menu Bar:	File (Select Printer)
Function Keys:	Not Available
Description:	Allows you to install a printer that can later be selected.
Procedure:	1. Select File at any point in your document.
	2. Choose Select Printer.
	3. Click on Add.
	4. A list of available printers drivers, found in the Printer Files directory, will appear. If the printer you want is not on the list, click on Change to change to the directory where the additional printers are located. Highlight the printer that you want to add, and click on Add.
	5. The printer driver name will appear, and you are prompted to approve or disapprove its selection. Click on OK.
	6. An informational message "Updating Fonts" appears; when WordPerfect is

through, you are returned to the Select
Printer screen. At this point you can select
the new printer by highlighting it and
clicking on Select, or you can click on
Close to return to your document without
selecting the new printer.

Note: Printers have different page defaults that
change the look of a completed document; select a printer before you create your document or else plan to spend a few moments after you have changed the printer making sure
that the margins and the fonts have not
changed significantly.

_____ *Printer, Selecting*

Menu Bar: File (Select Printer)

**Function
Keys:** Not Available

Description: Allows you to select another printer. The
printer must be installed before it can be
selected.

Procedure: 1. Select File at any point in your document.

2. Choose Select Printer.

3. The printer currently being used is
highlighted.

   a. Click on Add if the desired printer is
   not on the Select Printer display
   screen.

   b. Click on Windows Printer Drivers if
   you are changing to a Windows
   printer. Click on Setup if the desired
   printer is not on the Select Printer display screen.

4. Choose your new printer.

   a. If you are using WordPerfect, scroll through the list of printers until you come to the one you want. You may need to choose Change and use the WordPerfect printer diskettes to locate the printer you need.

   b. If you are using Windows, you may need to click on Add Printer and add the printer driver from diskette A: or B:. (You cannot use a WordPerfect printer driver for a Windows printer.)

5. Double-click on the new printer.

6. Click on OK to copy the printer driver and return to the Select Printer screen. The new printer is selected.

7. Click on Close to return to your document.

Notes:

1. The new printer setting is the new default; all documents created from this time forward will use the currently selected printer. Previously created documents will use the printer that was the default when they were created, and you will have to modify each file to accept the new printer. Removing a printer from the Select Printer screen has no effect whatsoever upon previously created documents.

2. It is better to choose the new printer before you start formatting your document since the fonts are printer dependent, as are some margins.

Printer Setup _____

Menu Bar: File (Select Printer)

**Function
Keys:**   Not Available

Description: Allows you to change printer options for this
                  document only.

Table 11.3. WordPerfect Printer Setup Defaults

Printer Driver	Your selection
Path for Downloadable Fonts and Printer	
Commands	None
Current Initial Font	Courier
Sheet Feeder	None
Destination Port	LPT1

Procedure: 1. Select File at any point in your document.

                  2. Choose Select Printer.

                  3. Click on Select. A dialog box appears that
                     allows you to change several printer set-
                     tings. Make whatever changes you need.

                  4. Click on OK to save the changes and re-
                     turn to the Select Printer screen.

                  5. Click on Close to return to your document.

_____ *Printer Setup (File Manager)*

Menu Bar: File (File Manager)

**CUA
Keyboard:**   Not Available

**WordPerfect
5.1 Keyboard:**   <F5>

Description: Allows you to set up a printer that the File
                  Manager will use.

Table 11.4. File Manager Printer Defaults

Windows Printer Defaults	
Printer	Your selection
Paper Source	Upper tray
Paper Size	Letter 8½″ × 11″
Orientation	Portrait
Scaling	100%
Copies	1

Options	
Print to	Printer
Job Timeout	0 Seconds
Margins	Default
Header	Download each job to Printer
Handshake	Hardware

Procedure: 1. Select File at any point in your document.

2. Choose File Manager.

3. Select File.

4. Click on Printer Setup.

5. A dialog box will appear that shows your current Windows (not WordPerfect) printer setup. Make any changes you need.

   a. To change options, click on the Options box.

   b. To add a printer, click on Add Printer. Tell the File Manager where the new driver is and click on OK.

6. Click on OK to save the changes and return to the File Manager.

7. Click on File/Exit File Manager to leave the File Manager window, or double-click

on the Control Menu icon (extreme upper left-hand corner).

Note: Unless you specify otherwise, WordPerfect files will use the printer drivers that they were created with and so will not need to use the Windows printer drivers.

See Also: *Print Manager* to disable the Print Manager in case of error messages.

Printing, Stop

See *Cancel Print Job.*

Selected Pages, Printing

See *Multiple Pages, Printing.*

Sheet Feeder

Menu Bar: File (Print, Select Printer)

Function Keys: Not Available

Description: Allows you to select a sheet feeder (which contains one or more paper bins and feeds paper to the printer one sheet at a time). You must have already installed a sheet feeder in order to select it here.

Procedure for Selecting a WordPerfect Sheet Feeder:

1. Select File at any point in your document.
2. Choose Select Printer.
3. Click on Setup.

4. Choose Sheet Feeder. Scroll through the list of sheet feeders until you come to the one you want.

5. Highlight the new sheet feeder.

6. Click on Select to save the change and return to the Printer Setup screen.

7. Click on OK to leave the Printer Setup screen and return to your document.

Procedure for Selecting a Sheet Feeder with Windows:

1. Select File when you are ready to print.

2. Choose Select Printer.

3. Click on Setup.

4. The Printer Dialog Box appears.

5. Scroll through the list of printers until you come to the sheet feeder you previously installed.

6. Change the paper source to reflect the new printer.

7. Click on OK to save the changes and return to the Setup screen.

8. Click on Close to return to your document.

Notes:

1. If the sheet feeder will not be using bin or tray 1, you will need to create a paper size definition so that the printer knows the location of the bin.

2. The new sheet feeder setting is the new default; all documents created from this time forward will use the new setting. Previously created documents will use the sheet feeder setting that was the default when they were created, and you will have to modify each document manually. Removing a sheet feeder from the Setup Menu has no effect upon previously created documents.

See Also: *Paper Size* (Chapter 4); *Printer, Installing.*

_____ *Soft Fonts*

See *Cartridges and Soft Fonts.*

_____ *Stop Printing*

See *Cancel Print Job.*

_____ *Text Print Quality*

See *Print.*

_____ *Windows Printer Drivers*

See Appendix A.

_____ *Word Spacing*

See *Printer Commands.*

_____ *WordPerfect Printer Drivers*

Menu Bar:	File (Select Printer)
Function Keys:	Not Available
Description:	Allows you to change, delete, add, or update your WordPerfect printer drivers.
Procedure:	1. Select File at any point in your document.
	2. Choose Select Printer.

3. Click on Select.

4. To add a printer, click on Add. To delete the currently highlighted printer, click on Delete. To copy a printer driver, click on Copy.

5. Click on OK to confirm your choices. Cancel to exit without making the change.

See Also: *Printer, Selecting.*

WordPerfect Printer Drivers, Modifying _____

Menu Bar: Not Available

**Function
Keys:**   Not Available

Description: Allows you to modify your WordPerfect printer drivers. This procedure is not guaranteed by WordPerfect.

Procedure: 1. Make a backup of the file you want to change, giving it a different name.

2. Type ptr/afc <Enter> at the MSDOS prompt where your WordPerfect printer driver files are located.

3. Press Retrieve (<Shift><F10>) and enter the name of the file you want to edit, or press List Files (<F5>) to list the available files; in that case, select the file and press <Enter>.

4. Change the file as needed.

5. Leave the Printer Program by pressing Exit (<F7>) or Quit (<Alt><F7>).

6. Save the file by pressing Y at the Save File prompt, or type a new filename and press <Enter>.

Note: WordPerfect does not guarantee that changed
.PRS files will do what you want them to and
will not replace a file you have destroyed. *Always* make a backup of the .PRS files before
you make changes to them.

Appendix A
WordPerfect and Windows

In order to join the Windows revolution, WordPerfect had to do certain things the Windows way, mainly in the matter of maneuvering around the desktop. This can be confusing for long-time WordPerfect users who already know how to maneuver around WordPerfect's desktop. Some of the old ways do not work at all any more; others take you to places you had never thought of going. (One of the problems with arriving someplace you had never thought of going is that you do not know how to leave.)

The Windows environment has caused other changes to WordPerfect that are supposed to be invisible to the user, but that have the result of making WordPerfect not-so-invisibly slower than it used to be. For one thing, WordPerfect now deals with Windows, which in turn deals with MS-DOS. For another, WordPerfect has had to become a graphical application to match Windows' graphical interface. (Graphical interfaces require more computer time than character-based interfaces.)

You can partially compensate for this slowness by utilizing Windows's HIMEM.SYS and SMARTDRV.SYS drivers or memory manager programs from other vendors and by installing additional memory into your computer. (SMARTDRV.SYS has some drawbacks. See the section called Windows Concepts for more information.)

This appendix will discuss:

- Windows Concepts, including system requirements.
- WordPerfect and maneuvering in Windows environments.
- Printing in Windows and WordPerfect.

Windows Concepts _____

Windows allows you to open several different applications and transfer information among them without having to close any of the applications. This means, for example, that it is easy to create a spreadsheet with one application and transfer all or part of it to WordPerfect via Spreadsheet Link, or to create a drawing in another application and quickly import it into a WordPerfect file. WordPerfect can import data from any Windows application that can support Dynamic Data Exchange (DDE), which is most of them.

Data are most frequently transferred from applications to WordPerfect through the Windows Clipboard, especially if the data in question will not need to be updated by the source application. (Clipboard is discussed in detail in the Windows Commands in the WordPerfect section that appears later in this appendix.)

Windows lets you switch among applications by reducing your current application to an icon and allowing you to open another. Then, when you want to return to your first application, you can reduce the second to an icon and restore the first. The application that is reduced to an icon will continue working in the background, and you have not spent the time involved in saving, closing, and exiting from an application.

See Also: Chapter 9 to import graphics.

Chapter 10 to import spreadsheets from any application, or data from DDE applications.

System Requirements _____

Before you installed Windows, your system had to meet certain specifications. WordPerfect has its own requirements above and beyond those of Windows. You cannot have too much memory for either application because, as mentioned earlier, graphical interfaces take up more memory than character-based applications.

- Trying to attract all the PC computer users in the world, Microsoft says that you can run Windows with an 8086 computer and 640KB of memory. (They do not say how happy you will be with Windows and the oldest computer on the market, though.) WordPerfect requires a computer with an Intel 80286, 80386, 80486, or higher processor chip and a minimum of 2MB memory that runs in Windows Standard or Enhanced Mode.

- Windows requires a monitor that is supported by it; WordPerfect requires an EGA, VGA, 8514A, or Hercules graphic board, all of which are supported by Windows.

- Both WordPerfect and Windows require a computer with at least one floppy drive and one hard disk with at least 6MB of memory.

- Both WordPerfect and Windows require printers that are supported by them if you plan to print through their applications. (You can print in WordPerfect even if Windows does not support the printer, and vice versa.)

- Neither WordPerfect nor Windows requires a mouse, but you cannot access all of either's features without one.

- WordPerfect requires Windows 3.0 or higher.

Basic Maneuvering in Windows

Windows, the program, is simple to use. Desktop windows are opened by double-clicking on their icons; an application within a window is opened by double-clicking on it. Applications and windows are closed by double-clicking on the Control Menu Box in the upper left-hand corner of every application/window. Other methods also exist for opening and closing applications, but these are the easiest and fastest. (Windows has 600 pages of documentation, not counting the glossary and index, that includes all sorts of how-to tips.)

Adding WordPerfect to a Group in the Program Manager

If you are going to use WordPerfect for Windows frequently, you can add it to an already existing group of related applications for more convenient access and a neater desktop. (WordPerfect creates a group that contains just WordPerfect applications.)

Procedure:
1. Open Windows.
2. Double-click on the Program Manager to open it.
3. Double-click on the group that contains the WordPerfect icons.
4. Double-click on the group that you want to add to WordPerfect.
5. Click and drag the WordPerfect icon from the old group to the new. The WordPerfect icon is transferred to the new group.
6. When you exit Windows, be sure to save your changes. Otherwise, the changes will not be there the next time you reenter Windows.

Notes:
1. The remaining icons (Speller, File Manager, Thesaurus) can still be accessed through WordPerfect, even though WordPerfect is no longer in the same group.
2. Other methods exist for adding Word-Perfect to other icons, but this is the quickest and easiest method.

Going to DOS

Description: Allows you to leave Windows temporarily to go to MS-DOS. You can return to Windows without having to reload the program.

Procedure: 1. At the Program Manager window, double-click on the Main Menu icon to open the window.

2. Double-click on DOS Prompt to temporarily leave the Windows environment. The DOS prompt appears.

3. When you are ready to return to Windows, go to the DOS prompt and type exit <Enter>. You will be returned to the Windows environment.

Opening WordPerfect

Description: Allows you to open the WordPerfect application.

Procedure: 1. At the Program Manager, double-click on the icon that contains the WordPerfect application.

2. Double-click on the WP logo. A blank screen appears, labeled WordPerfect—[Document1—Unmodified]. At this point, you can enter text or open an existing document.

Windows has other functions that play a large role in Word-Perfect functioning. They are covered in the section called Windows Commands in WordPerfect, which appears later in this appendix.

Maximizing Memory in Windows

Because memory is so important to speedy functioning of Windows and WordPerfect, Windows ships several drivers that are designed to increase the capabilities of your existing memory.

Windows is sold with an extended memory manager called HI-MEM.SYS, which prevents any two applications from using the same memory at the same time. When you install Windows, HIMEM.SYS is automatically installed in your CONFIG.SYS file, and no action is needed from you.

(Be careful with your HIMEM.SYS files. MS-DOS 5.0 also has a HIMEM.SYS file and it says that version supercedes the Windows 3.0 HIMEM.SYS. Always use the HIMEM.SYS with the latest date for best results, and remove the older ones.)

Windows also ships with the SMARTDrive disk-caching utility, which allows frequently used data to be kept in a special place for faster retrieval. SMARTDRV.SYS is also automatically placed in your CONFIG.SYS file when you install Windows.

There is no question that using SMARTDrive makes your Windows applications work much faster. The problem comes when you are working outside Windows; I have heard rumors of crashed disks because of SMARTDRV.SYS. In my own experience, some of the applications on my computer (such as MS-DOS WordPerfect 5.1) cannot be accessed if I have SMART-DRV.SYS enabled in my CONFIG.SYS file. If you are switching to Windows entirely and never plan to go to MS-DOS again, this is not a problem.

My solution, since I do have applications outside Windows, is to disable SMARTDRV.SYS whenever I need to, and then reboot the system. (I have to reinstall SMARTDRV.SYS and reboot, of course, before I go back to Windows.) Windows has a nifty feature that makes it easy and fast to modify the system files.

Another cheap solution for maximizing system memory in Windows is to get files off your hard disk as soon as possible and remove applications that you are no longer using (such as WordPerfect 5.1). Eventually, however, if your computer is having memory problems, you will need to upgrade your computer, either by purchasing a bigger, better, faster model or by adding additional memory to the computer you already have.

_____ *CONFIG.SYS File, Modifying*

Procedure: 1. From the Program Manager, double-click on the Main Menu.

2. Double-click on SysEdit.

3. Click on CONFIG.SYS.

4. To disable the SMARTDRV.SYS command line, add REM at the beginning of the SMARTDRV.SYS line. Do not put a space between REM and SMART.

5. Double-click on the Control Menu Box in the upper left-hand corner of the System Configuration Editor Dialog Box to close the SysEdit Menu.

6. Double-click on the Control Menu Box of the Main Menu to close the window.

Notes: 1. Even though you have changed the CON-FIG.SYS file, SMARTDRV.SYS will remain active until you reboot the computer. When you reboot, you will receive an error message about an unidentified command in the CONFIG.SYS file.

2. To enable the SMARTDRV.SYS command line, use a word processor or text editor or, if you have MS-DOS 5.X, its edit command, to remove the REM at the beginning of the SMARTDRV.SYS line. (You could go back to Windows to modify the CONFIG.SYS file, but that is not a quick procedure.) Then reboot.

_____ *Windows Commands in WordPerfect*

The following Windows commands can all be accessed through WordPerfect.

Cascade

Menu Bar:	Window
Function Keys:	Not Available
Description:	Allows you to arrange all the open windows so that their title bars show.
Procedure:	1. At any point in your document, select Window.
	2. Choose Cascade. All the windows are now arranged so that you can see the title bar of each.
	3. To return the windows to their original size, click on the Up Arrow box (upper right-hand corner) of the active window (the one with the color title bar).
Note:	If you find yourself hopelessly trapped with a bunch of small windows, try closing all but one. Then click on Window/Tile.
See Also:	*Control Menu Box; Tile.*

Clipboard

Menu Bar:	Edit
Function Keys:	Not Available
Description:	Allows you to place information in a central location for retrieval later. You can send information for retrieval by different applications. The information remains in the clipboard until you overwrite it or exit Windows.

Procedure for Sending Data to the Clipboard:

1. Highlight the data you want sent to the Clipboard.

2. Select Edit.

3. Click on Cut (if you want the data deleted from its current location) or Copy (if you only want a copy of the data sent to the Clipboard).

Procedure for Retrieving Data from the Clipboard:

1. Move the cursor to the point where you want the data to be placed.

2. Select Edit.

3. Click on Paste. The data are in the new location. The data are also still in the Clipboard, and will remain there until you overwrite or exit Windows (not WordPerfect).

Procedure for Viewing the Contents of the Clipboard:

1. Select the Control Menu Box in the upper left-hand corner of the screen.

2. Click on Switch To.

3. Highlight the Program Manager and click on Switch To.

4. Double-click on the Main Menu.

5. Double-click on the Clipboard icon.

Shortcut: The fastest way to view the contents of the Clipboard is to select Edit/Paste and see what appears on your screen. This can be messy, however, and I do not recommend that you try it unless you are certain that the Clipboard contents are not extensive.

Note: If you want to transfer data between applications, refer to the documentation of the two applications.

See Also: *DDE Link* (Chapter 10).

Control Menu Box _____

Menu Bar: Upper left-hand corner of screen

**Function
Keys:**   Not Available

Description: Allows you to exit an application quickly. You
                    can also use the Control Menu Box to move,
                    minimize, maximize, or resize the current
                    window, restore the window to its original di-
                    mensions, or switch to a different application.

Procedure: 1. Using the mouse, choose the Control
                       Menu Box.

                    2. Click on the option you want.

                    3. If you want to switch to a different
                       application,

                         a. Click on Switch To.

                         b. Highlight the open application that
                            you want to change to.

                         c. Click on Switch To.

Shortcuts: To minimize the current window, click on the
                    Down Arrow box in the upper right-hand cor-
                    ner; to maximize the current window, click on
                    the Up Arrow box in the upper right-hand
                    corner; to restore the window to its last set-
                    ting, click on the Up/Down Arrow box in the
                    upper right-hand corner. (The Down and Up
                    arrows affect the application window; the
                    Up/Down arrow affects only the document
                    window.)

Tile

Menu Bar:	Window
Function Keys:	Not Available
Description:	Allows you to position your windows so each window, not just the title bar, is visible.
Procedure:	1. At any point in your document, select Window.
	2. Choose Tile. All the open windows are now arranged so that you can see the contents of each one.
	3. To return the windows to their original size, click on the Up Arrow box (upper right-hand corner) of the active window (the one with the color title bar).
Note:	If you find yourself hopelessly trapped with a bunch of small windows, try closing all but one. Then click on Window/Tile.
See Also:	*Cascade; Control Menu Box.*

Printing

Both WordPerfect and Windows want you to print with WordPerfect's printer drivers. For one thing, if you format a document with a WordPerfect printer driver and then try to print the document with a Windows printer driver, the results may not reflect your intentions. Sometimes, however, you have good reason (color graphics and system fonts, for example) to use Windows. (Refer to Chapter 11 for a discussion of WordPerfect and Windows printer drivers.)

A word about terminology: You talk about printers; computer software talks about printer drivers. (A printer driver can drive more than one printer.)

File Manager

When you go into the printer setup screen from WordPerfect's File Manager, the printer selected is the one you installed when you set up Windows. The WordPerfect printer drivers are not selected and are not selectable. If you want to install the same printer drivers for both WordPerfect and Windows, you are going to have to install the same printer drivers twice, according to the appropriate directions.

Ordinarily, this difference in printer drivers should not matter if you are printing WordPerfect documents from the File Manager. The files should use the printer drivers they were created with (the WordPerfect printer drivers, for example) and bypass the Windows drivers completely. However, sometimes the documents will not print from the File Manager; instead, you will receive an error message that says "Can't Open Printer Device!" In this case, you will need to disable the Windows Print Manager.

Print Manager, Enable/Disable

Menu Bar:	Not Available
Function Keys:	Not Available
Description:	Allows you to enable or disable the Windows Print Manager in response to your printing needs.
Procedure:	1. Click on the Down Arrow in the extreme upper right-hand corner of the Word-Perfect window.
	2. Double-click on the Windows Main Menu.
	3. Double-click on Control Panel.
	4. Double-click on Printers.

5. Click on the Print Manager box at the bottom of the screen to change the toggle from On to Off, or vice versa.

6. Click on OK to save the change and return to the Control Panel window.

7. Double-click on the Control Menu Box (at the upper left-hand corner of the Control Panel window) to close the window and return to the Main Menu window.

8. Double-click on the Control Menu Box again to close the Main Menu window.

9. Your document should be on the desktop with the WP logo. Double-click on the WP logo to restore your document to the screen.

Installing Windows Printer Drivers

As with WordPerfect, you cannot select a printer that you have not already installed on the system.

Windows Printer Drivers, Installing

Menu Bar: From Windows

**Function
Keys:**   Not Available

Description: Allows you to add new or existing printer
                   drivers to your Windows environment.

Procedure: 1. From the Program Manager, double-click
                      on the Main Menu.

                   2. Double-click on the Control Panel.

                   3. Double-click on Printers.

4. Scroll through the list of available printer drivers.

   a. If the printer driver is already installed (copied to the system but not on the list of installed printers), click on Current in the Dialog Box.

   b. If you have a newer version of the existing printer driver, click on New. You will be prompted to insert the diskette that contains the driver.

   c. If the driver is not on the list but you have a printer driver diskette supplied by the printer manufacturer, click on Unlisted Printer at the end of the List of Printers box. You will be prompted to insert the diskette that contains the driver. Follow any special instructions listed by the printer manufacturer.

   d. Make sure, in the case of newer or unlisted printer drivers, that you have copied all associated files into the \SYSTEM subdirectory of the Windows main directory.

5. Choose Configure.

6. Click on the port to which you want to assign the new printer.

7. Click on OK to save the changes and return to the Printers Menu.

8. Click on OK to exit the Printers Menu and return to the Control Panel window.

9. Double-click on the Control Menu Box (at the upper left-hand corner of the screen) to leave the Control Panel and return to the Main Menu.

10. Double-click on the Control Menu Box again to close the Main Menu and return to the Program Menu.

Note: WordPerfect gives unguaranteed directions for modifying a WordPerfect printer driver. Windows gives no directions on modifying print drivers at all. If you modify printer drivers for either WordPerfect or Windows, be sure to make a backup of the printer driver first, in case something goes wrong with your modification. Neither WordPerfect nor Windows will replace a printer driver that you destroyed.

See Also: *WordPerfect Printer Drivers* (Chapter 11); *WordPerfect Printer Drivers, Modifying* (Chapter 11).

Glossary

Append: To attach to. WordPerfect uses this term when sending a copy of highlighted data to the Clipboard.

Cascade: A Windows term. Cascading allows you to see the title bars of all the open WordPerfect documents at once, with a corresponding reduction in window size. Contrast with *Tile*.

Clipboard: A Windows term. WordPerfect uses it to temporarily store data. Data remains in the Clipboard until it is overwritten or until you exit from Windows.

Control Menu Box: A Windows term and exclusive Windows function. A Control Menu Box is at the extreme left of every application title bar. Through the Control Menu Box, you can switch applications and manipulate the size of the currently open window.

Control Panel: A Windows term. The Control Panel, found in the Main Menu, is where you go to reconfigure your system

Disk-caching: A method of speeding up computer response time by saving frequently used data in one location. Whenever a data request is sent, the computer looks in the disk-caching location first. (Windows' SMARTDrive is a disk-caching utility.)

Driver: See *Printer Driver.*

Equation: A WordPerfect term. WordPerfect has an Equation Editor that helps you format scientific formulas and equations. Keep in mind, however, that the Equation Editor cannot help you formulate your equation; neither can it provide you with the correct answer.

File Manager: Both WordPerfect and Windows have a File Manager, and both are designed to help you organize your files and directories. WordPerfect's File Manager takes over many of the functions of the old List Files command, which is otherwise no longer available. The Windows File Manager does the same thing for Windows.

HIMEM.SYS: A Microsoft term. HIMEM is an extended memory manager found in Windows and MS-DOS 5.0 whose main job is to prevent any two applications from using the same memory at the same time.

Kerning: Kerning is the spacing of certain letter combinations, such as VA or MW. A kerned letter combination improves appearance by allowing one letter to overlap into the other's space.

Landscape: One of two printing choices. "Landscape" means that the text is printed sideways on the page; "Portrait" means that the text is printed vertically. "Portrait" is always the default printer setting.

Master Document: A collection of files into one document. The group of files can then be manipulated as a whole, rather than individually. It is much faster to generate a table of contents and index through a Master Document than it is to generate one index or table of contents for each chapter and then collate the tables and indexes manually.

Overstrike: A WordPerfect term that lets you type two characters on top of each other. The results depend upon your printer. Contrast with *Strikeout.*

Portrait: One of two printing choices. "Portrait" means that the text is printed vertically on the page; "Landscape" is printed sideways on the page. "Portrait" is always the default printer setting.

Printer Drivers: A set of software commands that tells the computer what kind of printer is attached and how the printer should behave.

Print Manager: A Windows term. The Print Manager manages the printing of files that are created in WordPerfect and sent to it.

Reveal Codes: Codes placed in WordPerfect documents (such as soft returns at the end of a line, or tabs) can be seen through the Reveal Codes feature although they do not show up on the Default or Draft Mode screens. Reveal Codes is invaluable in determining why a page does not format or print properly.

SMARTDrive: Windows's disk-caching utility. It can speed up Windows applications considerably, but some computers have difficulty using it.

Strikeout: Type that has been crossed out. ~~This is strikeout.~~ Contrast with *Overstrike.*

Styles: A collection of formatting commands that have been defined and named so that the style can be retrieved to a document. Styles is a big help in standardizing a collection of documents in a report or book.

Tile: A Windows term. Tile allows you to see the window (as opposed to the title bar) of every document that is open in WordPerfect.

Index

A

Advance, 210
ANSI Text, 77
Append
  defined, 259
  using, 81
Application, switching to, 253
Arabic Page Numbers, 127
ASCII Text, 77
Assign applications to menu, 56
Assign Applications. *See* File
  Manager Assign Applications.
Auto Redisplay, 26

B

Backup, using, 21
Backup Files, 37
Beep Options, 30
Beginning Font, 123
Beginning of document,
  keystrokes, 20
Binding Offset, 222
Block, 16
Block, Printing, 224
Block Protect, 81
Block, saving, 102
Bold
  keyboard shortcut, 19
  using, 105
Bottom of document, going to;
  keystrokes, 19
Boxes
  box position defaults, 191
  default settings, 190
Button Bar

described, 6
files, 37
using, 45

C

Cancel
  keyboard shortcut, 19
  using, 82
Cancel Print Job, 211
Capitalization, 107
Capitalization of Existing Text,
  109
Capitalization of New Text, 106
Cartridges and Soft Fonts, 212
Cascade
  defined, 259
  using in WordPerfect, 250
Center Line, 106
Center Page, 214
Center Page Top to Bottom, 214
Center Text, 106
Character sets
  keyboard shortcut, 19
  using, 146
Clear Screen, 46
Clipboard
  defined, 259
  retrieving data from, 251
  sending data to, 251
  using in WordPerfect, 250
  viewing contents of, 251
Close a file, 13, 47
Codes
  deleting, 85
  deletion, confirm, 30
  initial, setting, 33

setting for document, 47
See also Deleting Codes;
    Reveal Codes.
Color printing, 214
Colors
    text in Windows colors, 26
    draft mode, choosing, 29
    Reveal Codes, changing, 41
Columns
    display side by side, 26
    newspaper or parallel, 107
    shortcut method, 132
    table, 200
Compare Document, 52
Concordance, 159
Conditional End of Page, 83
CONFIG.SYS File, modifying for
    SMARTDRV.SYS, 249
Control Menu Box
    defined, 259
    using in WordPerfect, 252
Control Panel, defined, 259
Convert Case, 109
Convert from other Format, 48
Copy, keyboard shortcut, 19
Copy File, 50
Copy files, 58
Create Directory, 59
Cross-Reference, 160
Cut
    keyboard shortcut, 19
    using, 83

D

Dash, 136
Date
    automatically Inserting, 84
    format, 23
DDE Link
    linking two open files, 203
    linking unopened documents,
        203

Decimal Alignment Character,
    136
Default Mode, 54
Delete Block of Text, 83
Delete Files, 51
Delete to end of line, keyboard
    shortcut, 19
Deleting Codes, 85
Dialog boxes, 26
Directory
    changing, 24
    create, 59
    default , 25
    using, 25
Disk-caching, defined, 259
Display
    pitch, 110
    preferences, changing, 26
Document Comments, 52
Document Compare, 52
Document Defaults, 27
Document Files Location, 37
Document on Disk, printing
    from, 215
Document Summary
    creating, 86
    default settings, creating, 28
    using, 53
Document Window, 26
Double Indent, 117
Draft Mode
    colors, choosing, 29
    described, 7
    using, 12, 54

E

Endnote placement, determining,
    90
Endnotes, 88
Enter, 87
Envelopes, 87

Environment, changing, 30
Equations
    box defaults, 193
    box position defaults, 193
    changing default settings, 31
    defined, 260
    using, 192
Error Messages, understanding, 11
Exit WordPerfect, 14, 55

F

Fast Save, on/off toggle, 30
Figure
    box position defaults, 196
    box setting defaults, 195
    using, 195
File
    attributes, changing. *See* File Manager Attributes.
    closing, 14
    File Manager, deleting through, 60
    opening, 12, 73
    printing multiple, 221
    save to other format, 77
    saving, 13, 76
File Manager
    assign applications to menu, 56
    associate applications, 56
    attributes, 57
    copy files, 58
    defined, 260
    described, 7
    directory, create, 59
    files, delete, 60
    information, listing, 61
    information about system, 64
    layout, 68
    list files, 62

move/rename, 63
    Navigator, using, 64
    print, 65
    print Navigator window, 66
    printer setup, 236
    search, 67
    Viewer, 69
Files Location, 37
Find a File, 69
Find Words, 69
Flush Right, 111
Font
    attributes, setting, 1112
    changing (shortcut), 133
    choosing for printer, 216
    kerning, 119
Font, Initial, setting, 113
Fonts, Automatic Changes. *See* WordPerfect Printer Drivers.
Fonts, Soft, 212
Fonts, Substituting. *See* WordPerfect Printer Drivers, Modifying.
Footers, 92
Footnote/Endnote
    changing, 89
    creating, 88
    deleting, 89
    editing, 7
Force Odd/Even Page, 127
Format Document for Default Printer, 26
Forms
    printing, 218
    using, 91
Full Document, Printing, 222

G

Goto, 14
Graphic
    black and white, 26

files, 37
line, positioning defaults, 200
print quality, 222
retrieve without making
    changes, 196
retrieving to modify, 197

H

Hanging Paragraph, 114
Hard page break, keyboard
    shortcut, 19
Hard Return Character, 26
Hard Space, 136
Hard Tab, 136
Headers/Footers, 92
Height, 120
HIMEM.SYS, defined, 260
Hyphenation
    codes, 136
    file location, 37
    hyphenation zone, changing,
        116
    settings, 30
    using, 115

I

Import DDE Documents, 203
Import Spreadsheets, 205
Import Word Processing Files, 48
Indent, 116
Indent Left and Right, 117
Index, 161
Initial Codes, 33
Insert Page Number in Text, 127
Italics
    keyboard shortcut, 19
    using, 119
    See also Font Attributes.

J

Justification
    long method, 118
    shortcut, 134

K

Kerning
    defined, 260
    using, 119
Keyboard
    changing default, 34
    choosing, 8
    creating, 35
    file location, 37
    shortcuts, 19

L

Labels
    creating with Windows
        drivers, 183
    creating with WordPerfect
        drivers, 182
    default settings, 183
    using 181
Landscape
    defined, 260
    paper orientation, 100
    printing with, 219
    using, 219
    See also Paper Size.
Language, changing default, 36
Left and Right Margins, 123
Line
    draw, using, 197
    graphic, using, 199
Line Height, 120
Line Numbering, 121
Line Spacing
    shortcut, 135
    using, 122
Link
    DDE, using, 203
    spreadsheet options, setting,
        207
    spreadsheet, using, 206
List files. *See* File Manager List
    Files.

Lists, creating, 163
Location of Files, changing, 37
Locked Document, 73
Look Up function, 155
Lowercase, 109

M

Macro
  assigning to Button Bar, 165
  assigning to Macro Menu, 166
  converting from earlier
    formats, 167
  creating, 170
  editing, 170
  file location, 37
  playing, 169
  recording, 169
Margin Release, 123
Margins, 123
Marked Text
  define, 172
  generate, 173
  mark, 171
Master Document
  defined, 260
  expanding/condensing, 175
  subdocuments, adding, 174
Math functions. *See* Tables.
Memory, maximizing in
  Windows, 248
Menu settings, 30
Merge
  changing defaults, 38
  primary file, preparing, 185
  secondary file, preparing, 184
Move Text. *See* Copy or Cut.
Move/Rename File
  using with multiple documents
    63
  using with single documents
    71

MS-DOS, accessing, 247
Multiple files, printing, 221
Multiple pages, printing, 221

N

Navigator
  printing window, 66
  using, 64
New Page Number, 127
Normal text (type), keyboard
  shortcut, 19
Numbering, Line, 121
Numbering, Page, 127
Numbers, display and Entry, 26

O

Open a file, 11, 73
Outline
  creating, 95
  default options, 94
  numbering style, creating/
    changing, 94
  numbering, restarting, 95
  using, 94
Overstrike
  defined, 261
  using 125

P

Page Break, 126
Page Format, Suppress, 141
Page Numbering, 127
Page Number, Inserting, 127
Page Size and Type, Choose, 97
Page, Conditional End of, 83
Page, Force Odd/Even, 127
Page, Printing, 222
Paper Size, 97
Paragraph Numbering, 96
Password, 73
Paste

keyboard shortcut, 19
using, 99
Portrait
defined, 261
paper orientation, 99
See also Paper Size.
Position text on printed page,
210
Print
block, 224
color, 214
default settings, 222
File Manager, 65
full document, 222
graphics, 222
keyboard shortcut, 19
multiple pages, 222
whole document, 222
Print, Color, 214
Print, Double Sided, 225
Print, Full Document, 222
Print, Graphics, 222
Print, Page, 222
Print, Selected Pages, 222
Print Job, Cancel, 211
Print Manager
defined, 261
enable/disable, 226, 255
Print Multiple Files, 220
Print Multiple Pages, 221
Print Preview, 227
Print to Disk, 229
Printer
adding. *See* Printer: installing
commands, using, 230
deleting, 231
file location, 37
font, choosing, 216
initial settings, 39
initializing, 219
installing, 232
selecting, 233

Printer Commands, 230
"Printer device, can't open"
error message. *See* Print
Manager.
Printer Drivers
defined, 261
See also WordPerfect Printer
Drivers
Printer Setup
File Manager, 235
WordPerfect, 234
Printing, landscape, 219
Printing, Stop, 211
Protect Block, 81

Q
Quick List, 75

R
Redline
method, 128
using, 129
Replace, 149
Retrieve File, 75
Reveal Codes
colors, changing, 41
defined, 261
explained, 9
using, 100
window, changing size, 101
Roman Page Numbers, 127
Rows, Table, 200
Ruler Bar
columns, 131
explained, 10
font and size, 132
justification, 133
settings, 30
size, 132
spacing, 134
styles, 134

tab, 135
tables, 136
toggle, 130
Save
block, 101
file, 12, 76

S

Save As, 77
Save File to Earlier WordPerfect
    Version, 77
Scroll Bar settings, 26
Search
    file manager, 67
    next occurrence, 152
    previous occurrence, 153
    using, 15, 151
Select, 16
Selected Pages, Printing, 221
Sheet Feeder
    selecting with Windows
        drivers, 238
    selecting with WordPerfect
        drivers, 237
SMARTDrive.SYS
    defined, 261
    using, 248
Soft Fonts, 212
Sort
    block of text, 187
    defaults, 186
    file, 187
Spaces, Underline, 145
Spacing. *See* Line Spacing; Line
    Height.
Special Codes, 137
Speller
    file location, 37
    using, 153
Spreadsheet
    file location, 37

importing, 205
link options, 207
linking, 206
Status Bar display
    measurements, 26
Stop Printing, 211
Strikeout
    defined, 261
    using, 129
Styles
    defined, 261
    file location, 37
    using, shortcut, 134
Style Sheet
    creating, 138
    editing, 139
    using with existing text, 140
    using with uncreated text, 139
Subscript, 141
Suggest spelling choice, 153
Summary, 53
Superscript 140
Suppress Page Format, 141
System requirements, discussed,
    244

T

Table of Authorities
    discussed, 176
    formatting defaults, setting, 42
    referenced, 159
    using, 176
Table of Contents, 178
Tables
    math, using with, 202
    setting defaults, 201
    using, 200
    using, shortcut, 136
Tabs, Set
    codes, 136
    setting, 142

underline, 145
using, shortcut, 136
Text
  append, 81
  marking for lists, 171
  position on printed page, 210
  selecting, 17
  undelete, 18, 104
  undo, 18, 104
  Windows colors, 26
Text print quality, 222
Thesaurus
  file location, 37
  using, 155
Tile
  defined, 262
  using in WordPerfect, 253
Top and Bottom Margins, 123
Type size, changing, 143
Type, Italic, 118
Type, Special Characters. *See*
  WordPerfect: character sets.
Type, Superscript, Subscript, 140
Type, Underline, 145
Typeover, 102
Typesetting. *See* Printer
  Commands.

U

Undelete, 17, 103
Underline
  keyboard shortcut, 19
  spaces, 145
  tabs, 145
  using, 145
Underline, Double. *See*
  Underline; Font Attributes.
Undo, 17, 103
  allow, 30
  keyboard shortcut, 19
Units of Measure, 26

V

View, 78
Viewer, using in File Manager,
  69

W

Widow/Orphan, 104
Window, 18
Windows
  Cascade, using in WordPerfect,
    250
  Clipboard, using in
    WordPerfect, 250
  commands in WordPerfect,
    249
  concepts discussed, 244
  Control Menu Box, using in
    WordPerfect, 252
  maneuvering in, 245
  memory, maximizing, 247
  opening WordPerfect in 247
  printer drivers, installing, 255
  Tile, using in WordPerfect, 253
Word Count, 156
WordPerfect
  character sets keyboard
    shortcut, 19
  character sets, using, 146
  concepts discussed, 6
  exit from, 14, 55
  getting started, 11
  icon, adding to Windows
    Program Group, 246
  maneuvering in, 14
  new features, 6
  opening from Windows, 247
  printer drivers, 239
  printer drivers, modifying, 240
Word Processing Applications,
  Saving to, 77
Word Spacing, 230